Last to First

LAST TO FIRST

The Story of the Mets

LARRY FOX

Foreword by Lindsey Nelson

An Associated Features Book

1817

HARPER & ROW, PUBLISHERS

NEW YORK, EVANSTON, AND LONDON

*To Mrs. Payson and all the Met fans who suffered so long.
And to Mrs. Fox, who suffered, too.*

ACKNOWLEDGMENTS

To Bill Shea, for getting us all a ball club to root for and write about and for making his memories and his files on those early struggles available; and also to Joe McDonald, director of minor-league operations for the Mets, a special word of thanks for his time. Also appreciation to Matt Winick of the Mets, Joe Reichler of the Baseball Commissioner's office, the Elias Sports Bureau, and to Barney Kremenko, who was there, too.

Contents

x / Contents

FOREWORD
by Lindsey Nelson

I could hear the World Series crowd at Shea Stadium roaring on every pitch. I could hear them, but I couldn't see them. It was October 16, 1969. The Baltimore Orioles were batting in the top of the ninth. The New York Mets were leading, 5-3. I was standing now, alone, in the far corner of the washroom, beyond the Mets' locker room on the ground floor. I had been at the NBC microphone doing the television play-by-play for an audience of millions until the eighth inning when the Mets had gone ahead. Then I had run out of the booth, down the ramps, heading for what I knew would be a wild locker room scene. For the first time, I hadn't trusted the elevators. Frantically, I envisioned the Mets celebrating the magical moment while I was stuck somewhere in an overcrowded elevator. No chance! That's why I had raced down the ramps, and now I was getting my breath, and a sobering shock at the same time. As I contemplated the moment, the realization came upon me fully. "The METS," I thought, "are about to be the champions of the WORLD!"

I wasn't alone in that thought. Thousands of people in Manhattan, with the same realization, were about to pour forth into the city streets—laughing, crying, dancing, tossing tons of confetti, newspapers, ticker tape, phone books into the air. Soldiers in Vietnam and Thailand were hanging onto every word of the overseas broadcast. Cab drivers all across this land pulled over to curbs to listen. Schoolchildren with smuggled transistors squealed uncontrollably in classrooms.

"There's one man out," somebody shouted to me. The network technicians had a platform ready in the center of the locker room. The camera was trained on it. The microphones were in position. There was the Telex ready to be stuck into my ear. The stage managers had the cue cards ready.

I remembered the first game the Mets ever won, an exhibition game over the Cardinals in Saint Petersburg when Manager Casey Stengel had gone to his bench for a pinch-hitter named Choo Choo Coleman, and Choo-Choo had hit a home run. He didn't hit many more.

I remembered the first National League game the Mets ever played. It was in St. Louis against the Cards, and Roger Craig was the Met pitcher. With a man on third, he committed a balk. The first run ever scored against the Mets came home on a balk.

There was Old-Timers' Day at the Polo Grounds that summer of 1962. And the Dodgers beat the Mets, 17-3. I remembered Bill Terry that night, shaking his head and saying, "I just don't know if I could stand that."

"There are two men out," yelled a voice from the locker room. I straightened my tie and went out to the platform, where a television monitor showed the scene outside. Cautiously, I put my wristwatch into my pocket.

There was a night when I had broadcast a Met game without a monitor. I had been in a cage suspended from the very top of the Astrodome in Houston, 208 feet directly over second base. I was in fair territory, but I was safe. The Mets of that year weren't hitting balls 208 feet in any direction, not even straight up. I was up there for four hours, and my only form of communication was a walkie-talkie on a wave length that was mixed up with a local taxicab company's. The Mets lost.

I remembered Marv Throneberry hitting what looked like a triple, only he missed first and second on the way around and was called out on an appeal play. Rod Kanehl, in windblown Candlestick Park in San Francisco, racing from his post at third base back down the left-field line for a pop fly that fell untouched behind first base. Ron Swoboda racing in on a ground ball to the outfield with the bases loaded and swinging his glove down in full flight like Willie Mays only coming up empty, with three runs scoring while the ball rolled to the fence. The pain on Manager Wes Westrum's face almost any day.

Lindsey Nelson helps Casey Stengel celebrate
his seventy-second birthday at the Polo Grounds in 1962,
the Mets' first season.

Those had been painful years for the Mets, the Met fans, and
the Met broadcasters. The Mets had become a symbol of ineptitude,
a national joke. While they endured it, it was a role they did not
relish. The Met fans endured and multiplied. They cheered and
yelled and hoped and prayed—and often they laughed to keep from
crying. Bad jokes were made by people who misunderstood and
mistakenly thought the Met fans cherished a loser.

But this year had been so different. Manager Gil Hodges had
managed to instill quiet dignity and confidence. It had been con-
tagious. The Mets had the best pitching. They made all the plays.
The defense was unbelievable. They topped the Cubs and the

Cards, they swept the Braves, lost the opener to the Orioles, and were now on the verge of making four straight in the World Series.

On the monitor, I watched the last out being made, heard the Mets proclaimed World Champions, saw fans race onto the field, digging up the turf of Shea Stadium, hurling handfuls of dirt high into the air.

The locker room door burst open, and the Mets stormed jubilantly in. It was absolute bedlam. Champagne corks popped. Somebody was pouring champagne over the head of the Mayor of New York, and the Mayor was pouring it on somebody else. Somebody was pouring it on me and my microphone. I felt sticky champagne in my hair, cold champagne running down my neck inside my shirt. My eyes burned with stinging champagne so that I could hardly keep them open, and I didn't care. My pockets and my watch were soaked.

But the New York Mets were the World Champions!

They had been through seven years of famine, absolute famine. Because of those years, this year of plenty was magnified a thousandfold.

From the day they were born, I broadcast almost every game the Mets ever played. I used to say, not entirely facetiously, that my job was hardest—I didn't have to play the games, I had to explain them. Now all I had to do was applaud, and laugh, and soak up the magic of this moment that could never ever possibly be duplicated.

It's a trite and inadequate word, but it was "beautiful"—the most beautiful thing that ever happened in the world of sports.

Introduction:
Meaning of a Miracle

America talks in many voices, and through the 1960s these were mostly voices of anger: wars, riots, the cries for social changes and the cries against. A decade for conflict.

It wasn't surprising that the growing sport during these ten years was professional football, an activity in which unbridled violence is put on display under only the most minimal of controls.

Baseball was almost an anachronism during these years. Baseball, for all its hidden viciousness, its bean balls and takeout slides at second base, is a mannered game played at a leisurely pace. The rules have not changed for years, and neither have the basic techniques. New cities are added only with reluctance. In this comfortable establishment game, the greatest moment was opening day when the President threw out the first ball.

But in 1969 all this changed. A young team of New York Mets did it. They revived baseball and made Americans speak for a few months, at least part of the time, in one voice. How did they accomplish this miracle of bringing Wall Street bankers and Greenwich Village hippies to their feet at the same instant chanting, "Let's go, Mets"? They did it by challenging the establishment while still remaining a part of it . . . and by winning. They didn't challenge the establishment of baseball, only the establishment figures. The fat Cardinals were defending champions, the prestigious Orioles had the unbeatable veteran stars, Leo Durocher was the world's greatest manager, according to Dad.

The Mets beat them all, and young America and the nation's

underdogs took them to heart. And because these brash youngsters were winning within the framework of baseball—three outs to an inning and all that—and winning under the guidance of a manager who played by the book, their older fans could accept them, too.

This may have been the real miracle.

The rise of the Mets took place, of course, in New York, a city exemplifying the anger and divisiveness of the nation. As the Mets were making their surge to a pennant, New Yorkers were involved in a bitter municipal election. Sure as right-handed hitters do better against left-handed pitchers, the Mets played a role in deciding the outcome.

On Thursday morning, October 16, 1969, John V. Lindsay knew where he was going. He was on his way to be re-elected mayor of New York. A baseball team was going to help him do it. Once he had complained, "Do I have to go out to the ball park again?" But now he realized that Shea Stadium, home of the New York Mets, was the focus of the nation and of his city.

Ten months earlier the New York Jets of the American Football League had stunned the world by upsetting Baltimore in the Super Bowl. Their 16-7 victory had inspired a brief orgy of civic pride, but the Jets' triumph was a sudden, one-day affair. One Sunday morning they were 18-point underdogs. That night they were champions. The Mayor was almost ignored when he welcomed the team back from Miami at the airport, and he was booed when he tried to introduce the Jets at a City Hall reception. He never was really part of their victory.

With the Mets, though, it was different. They had started the long season 100-to-1 underdogs in the National League, but by midseason New York fans began to realize this would be the best Met team ever. In late summer, when they staged a dramatic rush to overhaul the pace-setting Chicago Cubs, interest and excitement began to build. After the Mets clinched the Eastern Division championship with eight days left in the season, the fever reached every corner of the city. Now there would be a playoff to decide the National League pennant and then, finally, the World Series.

At each plateau, the hysteria exploded anew as eight million New Yorkers suddenly found a common bond and the nation joined in cheering these glorious one-time street urchins of baseball.

Crime in the streets? Ha! The only crimes were on the basepaths, committed by umpires and opponents of the home team. Genera-

Rod Gaspar douses Mayor Lindsay with champagne as the Mets celebrate their World Series victory.

tion gaps? Look how manager Gil Hodges, the big bear of a father figure, handled his youthful tribe. Dirty sidewalks? Toss some more ticker tape, Charlie, the Mets are winning again. New York's problems hadn't been solved, they were merely obscured for a few brief weeks under a huge euphoric cloud and nobody even bothered with a smog warning. For a few brief weeks, life was simple again and our troubles could be made to disappear, like Leo Durocher and his swaggering Cubs. If only the rest of the world had Mets to call their own.

Mayor Lindsay and his advisers grasped this cultural phenomenon and made it theirs. On earlier campaign trips, disgruntled voters had thrown beer at the Mayor. But when the Mets beat the Atlanta Braves three straight for the National League pennant, Met players poured champagne on Lindsay's head when he visited their clubhouse. The difference was more than price and vintage. Not for a million dollars could the Mayor have staged a scene to present himself in a more sympathetic setting. And now there was a chance it would happen again.

On this particular Thursday morning, the Mets held a 3-to-1 advantage over Baltimore's Orioles in the World Series. One more victory and they would be World Champions. "We've given hope to every underdog in the world," said Ron Swoboda, who had been a Met when that word produced laughter, not applause. And Mayor Lindsay, a jeered-at underdog himself when his re-election campaign began, meant to be there when they popped the corks for the big one.

As the ninth inning began, the Mets held a 5-3 lead and the Mayor's party began to edge forward in its seats as sharp-eyed aides noted the quickest and safest route to the home team's clubhouse. Jerry Koosman walked Frank Robinson, which brought the tying run to the plate, and when the tying run is huge Boog Powell, that means one swing can make the game start all over. But Powell hit a grounder to Al Weis at second, and Robinson was forced. Then Brooks Robinson hit a fly ball to Ron Swoboda in deep right field, and the Mets were only one out away from the championship. The next batter was Dave Johnson, the count went to two balls, one strike, and he hit the fourth pitch to deep left field. Cleon Jones drifted back to the warning track in front of the fence, thinking all the time, "Come down. Come on down, baby. I got you."

Ed Charles jumps with joy and his face
mirrors his happiness as Jerry Koosman embraces
catcher Jerry Grote after the final out
in the World Series makes the Mets World Champions.

And at 3:17 in the afternoon the Mets were indeed World Champions. After the division- and pennant-clinching victories, Met fans had descended on the field and torn it to shreds, ripping up sod, tearing down portions of the outfield fence, stealing bases, home plate, the pitcher's rubber. Today, with a little less exuberance, they went at it again, almost by rote. Police stopped fans trying to make away with entire seats, an usher was belted and carried off on a stretcher, and a young fan plopped a huge piece of sod in the ample lap of Mrs. Charles Shipman Payson, 65-year-old multimillionaire owner of the Mets. (Nonplused only temporarily, she gave it to her chauffeur for planting in the lawn of one estate or another.) And downtown, a blizzard of paper showered down from Manhattan's huge office buildings. An all-time record, the Department of Sanitation declared. Who was this guy Lindbergh, anyway? Augmenting the ticker tape was that symbol of today the computer punch card.

Underneath Shea Stadium, in the Mets' clubhouse, another celebration was taking place. Gil Hodges' office, to the left as you enter the home clubhouse, was crowded but quiet, reflecting the man—so controlled and self-sufficient, his emotions always sealed below the surface.

But down the hall was bedlam. Here and there some of the older players silently sipped their champagne straight from the bottle, only their eyes revealing their happiness. But the body of this Met team wasn't of champagne vintage. This was the now generation. You don't sip fine wine in time to a rock beat. Champagne? It tickles your nose as a drink and burns your eyes as a shampoo. The corks are for popping and exploding across the room; the bottles are for shaking; the pale-gold liquid for squirting in a frothy mess. Just like they used to do with soda pop as kids not so long ago. Reporters and club officials, who knew enough to get in out of the champagne, entered the dressing room in tightly buttoned raincoats.

On a platform erected in the middle of the floor stood television announcer Lindsey Nelson, his clothes wet and his collar wilted from repeated showers of champagne. One by one, players hoarsely screamed their delight into his microphone as millions in New York and around the nation watched and grinned. And as the heroes shouted and hugged each other, a dozen women attempted to make sense of the spectacle from the periphery of the crowd. Most of them were wives of team owners and officials, breaching for the first time the male sanctity of a World Series clubhouse. That's the kind of victory this was, and soon Pearl Bailey was in the room, singing and dancing with third-baseman Ed Charles. Miss Bailey had adopted the Mets. The night before, some of the Baltimore players had attended her performance of *Hello, Dolly!* She introduced them to the audience, then gibed at the enemy: "What are you guys doing here, anyway? The way you've played the last few days, you should be home rehearsing."

A short, plump woman was assisted up onto the platform. Mrs. Payson, the only woman president of a major-league baseball team. "Oh my, oh my, oh my," she said, thrilled beyond words. From the beginning, she had been the Mets' biggest stockholder and their biggest fan, her floppy hats almost a fixture in a box seat near the home-team dugout.

Off in one corner, Mary Lindsay, the Mayor's wife, stood with a tolerant half smile, as if watching free-play period at a progressive nursery school. Her husband soon made his way to the platform. Grinning and disheveled, he was unintelligible to those in the room. But who cared? Most of them couldn't vote in New York anyway. What counted were the television viewers at home who could hear —and see—the candidate in company with their heroes. Rod Gaspar, a substitute outfielder who had doused the Mayor at the pennant-clinching, jumped on the platform to repeat his role. Up went the champagne bottle as if in a tribal ritual and out gushed the bubbly over His Honor's head. But then the Mayor grabbed the bottle himself. Deliberately and with timing worthy of Laurel and Hardy, he raised the bottle, tilted it, and doused Gaspar in return as the room rocked with laughter and delight. The player sputtered and wiped his eyes and, at this moment, a skinny twenty-three-year-old rookie from Long Beach, California, with a .228 batting average, was helping elect a mayor of New York.

*"Know how sublime
a thing it is to
suffer and be strong."*
—LONGFELLOW

Last to First

They Called Him George

It was, on the surface, just another preseason exhibition game between major-league teams in Long Beach, California. The Chicago Cubs and the Cleveland Indians, both of whom trained in Arizona, were picking up a little extra money. It was a Sunday afternoon, March 20, 1966, and Nels Burbrink, new scout in southern California for the New York Mets, was in the stands long before game time. Maybe he knew something.

As the Indians were taking batting practice a youngster unlisted on any program warmed up in the bullpen. Burbrink could see he was throwing hard, and when the kid was brought in to pitch to some Cleveland regulars, Burbrink, a former catcher, hunched forward to get a better look. The fans didn't know who this youngster was, but Burbrink did. The kid's name was Tom Seaver. He was a free agent, and the Indians were trying him out to see if he would be worth bidding for in a $40,000 lottery. Burbrink also was wondering about this. Seaver didn't know it—and neither did the Indians—but he was trying out for the Mets, too.

In his brief batting practice session, Seaver pitched to three hitters—Max Alvis, a tough veteran third-baseman and right-handed hitter who had belted twenty-one home runs the previous season; Fred Whitfield, a left-handed power-hitting first-baseman who had batted .293 with twenty-six home runs; and George Banks, a free-swinging rookie who batted right and was getting a chance in the big leagues after socking thirty-five homers in Portland.

Burbrink was astounded. The year before, he and most scouts

had labeled Seaver, then a sophomore at the University of Southern California, "no more than an $8,000 player, at best." Burbrink knew the heavy-shouldered right-hander had been improving. In reports to his new club, the Mets, he had raised Seaver's bonus value during the spring to $12,000 and then to $15,000 and finally to $25,000.

But that day in Long Beach he saw a fast ball Seaver had never shown before. "I saw some smoke," Burbrink said as he rushed his report to his immediate superior, Bing Devine. Burbrink conceded that veteran players hate to attack an unknown rookie with confidence because they fear his possible wildness, but the scout pointed out that "Whitfield was the only one to hit one or two of Seaver's fast balls with any authority."

Burbrink said the Mets should go the $40,000 for Seaver's services. Devine, assistant to the president of the Mets, agreed. But his boss, George M. Weiss, was reluctant. Weiss was relying on the older reports and did not think Seaver was worth the money. And he couldn't be blamed for being a little dubious about the new man's rave report. He also had to be aware that Devine was the person who had hired Burbrink. On March 24, only four days after Seaver's supposedly secret workout with the Indians, Devine composed a three-page single-spaced memo to Weiss pleading for permission to bid for Seaver. Time was of the essence. A decision had to be made within a week.

George Thomas Seaver had received his first line in professional baseball's archives back in June of the previous year, 1965. As a student at the University of Southern California he was drafted by the Los Angeles Dodgers. But he didn't care much for the Dodger organization and declined the small bonus they offered to continue his college education. So on January 29, 1966, his name was thrown back in the pot, and he was selected again in a special drawing, this time by the Atlanta Braves. And this time he signed with the National League team's Richmond, Virginia, farm club. The date of the signing was February 24, which was important. So was his $40,000 bonus, payable $25,000 the first year and $15,000 the second. (Even then, at twenty-one, the open-faced but computer-minded Seaver knew about taxes and such.)

Within four days of the signing, though, Jess Hill, the long-time athletic director at Southern Cal, had sent off an indignant letter to Baseball Commissioner William D. Eckert. He pointed out that the Trojans already had played two games before the 24th—Feb-

George Thomas Seaver . . . out of a hat.

ruary 11 against California State Poly and February 19 against San Fernando State—and that the Braves were violating baseball rules by signing Seaver after his college season had begun. Hill's long letter concluded: "George Seaver is the outstanding member of the team. He requested of the university and was granted substantial assistance to attend the spring semester. His signing and leaving the university would be an act unfair to the university, his teammates and college baseball. We would appreciate hearing from you as to his status."

Faced with this angry letter, Eckert had to act, and he quickly called a hearing in Miami Beach. Seaver and his father, Charles, a former Walker Cup golfer, were contacted, and so were officials at Southern Cal and the Pacific Eight Conference. John Mullen, farm director of the Braves, was called in and explained that his organization thought the two games in question had been merely "practice" exhibitions. Eckert, however, ruled the Braves had acted illegally. Their Richmond club was fined $500, and Seaver was declared a free agent.

This was far from the end of it, though. The ruling left Seaver in limbo. Although he had received none of the bonus money, he was still considered a professional because he had signed the contract. His college career was over, and yet he could not just go out and sign with any other club. He had to wait until the next professional draft in June. What if he suffered some disabling injury in the meantime? Seaver had signed with the Braves in good faith—what was baseball going to do about him? You didn't have to be a lawyer to see all the ramifications of this one.

After failing in attempts to have Seaver's eligibility and scholarship restored, Eckert huddled with his staff once again. Their Solomon-like decision: Seaver would be put up in a lottery, like a new car or a two-week vacation to Bermuda, among any teams willing to match the Braves' original $40,000 contract. The Braves, of course, were excluded, and a wire explaining the rules in this game of baseball bingo was sent out to the other nineteen teams on March 16. The deadline for entering was April 1.

The Philadelphia Phillies and the Cleveland Indians quickly responded and, as the deadline approached, it began to look as if only two teams were going to bid for young Seaver.

The dispute within the Mets' family was a basic one, going far beyond the question of a $40,000 pitcher. Weiss was the old conservative president of the Mets. Vaughan P. (Bing) Devine had been brought in a year earlier as his eventual successor, but now Weiss had suddenly delayed his retirement. Devine was young, dynamic, and eager to get on with running the club. As April 1 drew near, he continued his selling job on Weiss.

He succeeded just in time, which was standard procedure when anyone dealt with Weiss. The canny old executive always waited until the last minute to meet a deadline, whether in bidding for players, in making trades, or in sending in rosters. This had been his pattern as boss of the Yankees, when he could afford it; and as boss of the Mets, when he could not. "Why not use all the time they give you?" he'd say. "You never can tell what will happen."

The Mets sent their wire to the commissioner's New York office just before the close of the working day of April 1, making it three clubs that wanted a shot at Seaver—the Mets, the Phils, and the Indians.

The next morning was the kind of spring day the Florida Chamber of Commerce immodestly describes as typical, bright and sunshiny, when two baseball executives drove down from Fort Lauderdale, Florida, to Miami Beach to see their boss, the commissioner. Eckert was a retired air force lieutenant-general who found himself completely out of place away from the uniformed bureaucracy that had been his life. The General's two top aides, assigned to guide him in a world he didn't understand, were Lee MacPhail and Joe Reichler.

MacPhail, a pleasant, round-faced man, had been general manager of the Baltimore Orioles. His father, Larry, had owned three different major-league teams. Lee's title was "Administrator." He ran the shop. Reichler had been a respected baseball writer for the Associated Press for many years. Now he handled the General's public relations. He was never far away.

Reichler and MacPhail lived in Fort Lauderdale during the spring training period and drove to the General's suite in the Flamingo Courts quite regularly. As they headed down this morning, they chatted about several items of business they would have to discuss with the commissioner. The Seaver matter was considered too trivial even for this kind of small talk, Reichler would recall later.

Eventually Tom Seaver would be the young man who single-handedly started the bumbling Mets on the upward road from chumps to champs. But on this day, April 2, 1966, he was still just another kid pitcher. "When we did get around to him, we called him George," Reichler said with a smile.

After MacPhail and Reichler wound up their more important business with the commissioner in his hotel suite they decided to complete the drawing for Seaver before lunch. Reichler took three scraps of paper and appropriately labeled them. He was the only one of the three with a hat handy, so he took off his white sun cap and dropped in the three slips. As Reichler held the cap by the bill, Eckert picked out "Mets." The next day Burbrink signed Seaver to a contract.

These events produced no headlines in New York or anywhere else. But George, or Tom, Seaver was on his way, and so were the Mets.

2

Shea Wasn't Always a Stadium

One afternoon before a pre-season exhibition game in Brooklyn, Yankee Manager Casey Stengel was trying to show Mickey Mantle, then a rookie, how he used to play the tricky wall in Ebbets Field. When Mantle appeared dubious about the old man's credentials, Casey snapped back angrily, "Well, I wasn't born sixty years old, you know." Likewise, the Mets weren't born the day they happened to win title to Tom Seaver in a lottery.

The Met story really begins in 1952, in Boston, where the seventh-place Braves drew less than 300,000 fans and were about to surrender the city to the American League Red Sox.

That same year, the Braves signed a twenty-year-old infielder for their Class-C farm team in Quebec. He hit .317 as a rookie, but it still would take Ed Charles ten years to make the majors.

Lou Perini, president of the Braves, was looking for a new home for his franchise and he settled on Milwaukee. When he drew almost two million fans his first year in the new city—and passed that figure the following season—baseball's first modern franchise shift was rated a success. The floating franchise was born and the old rigid framework permanently breached. Soon after this, friends of Walter O'Malley's, portly president of the Brooklyn Dodgers, noted a faraway gleam in his eye.

The Dodgers were one of the National League's cornerstone franchises and, since World War II, one of its most successful. But

7

Branch Rickey (left) and Bill Shea after Rickey is named
president of the Continental League.

O'Malley realized that with a small stadium (32,000-plus capacity)
and limited parking facilities he had just about reached his maximum return. With three teams (the Yankees, the Dodgers, and the
Giants) all sharing the same market, there also was a ceiling on
television revenue.

New York's other National League team, the Giants, was a more
compelling hardship case, although this, too, was relative. The
Giants had been consistently in the black financially, but they were
doing poorly on the field and could see trouble ahead. Their stadium, the Polo Grounds, was almost twice as big as Ebbets Field,
but in worse condition and in a worse location.

The West Coast was vast and growing virgin territory, and pay-
television interests in California joined the siren chorus. Although
both O'Malley and Horace Stoneham, hereditary owner of the

Giants, denied they were committed to the move, by 1957 both teams had received permission from their National League peers to head for the West Coast if they wished.

That June, an all-round athlete graduated from Morehouse College in Atlanta, where he had earned twelve varsity letters. Given the choice of signing with the Harlem Globetrotters or the New York Knicks in pro basketball, the Cleveland Browns in pro football, and the Pittsburgh Pirates in pro baseball, Donn Clendenon picked the Pirates.

The city of New York was officially indifferent and snubbed O'Malley's plea for a new stadium site in downtown Brooklyn. The city offered instead some municipal property in Flushing Meadow, Queens.

Many in the city were, however, alarmed, and one of these was George V. McLaughlin, a politically oriented banker from Brooklyn. McLaughlin's bank, the Brooklyn Trust Company, had been the admistrator of the debt-ridden Dodgers for the old McKeever and Ebbets estates. In the two decades before World War II those famous Brooklyn fans were loud but very few in number.

During this period of the Dodgers' travail, McLaughlin had as protégés three young lawyers: Jim McLoughlin, William A. Shea, and Walter O'Malley. Later, Bill Shea was to recall, "It was George V. who set O'Malley up with the Dodgers. He could have tapped any one of the three of us for the job. But O'Malley was the oldest and was more interested in business than in the practice of law. So he got in . . . and gradually took over."

Now that O'Malley and the National League were about to desert his hometown, McLaughlin attempted to halt the exodus. He made overtures to purchase one of the departing teams and actually submitted a firm bid of over $2 million for the Giants. Acting for McLaughlin in most of these endeavors was his old protégé Bill Shea, now a successful corporation lawyer with strong political ties of his own. (Jim McLoughlin, third member of the triumvirate, and no relation to their mentor, had become an outstanding trial lawyer.)

As O'Malley and Stoneham played games with their long-time fans about whether they really and truly intended to move, Warren C. Giles, president of the National League, played the same game with McLaughlin and Shea. Baseball Commissioner Ford C. Frick meanwhile sat by, agreed that it would be a shame for New York not to be represented in the National League, and repeated his favorite apologia, "It's a league matter."

On October 7, 1957, during the World Series, when fans and press might be distracted, the Dodgers and Giants announced their move to California. Handsome new stadia would be built for them by the cities of Los Angeles and San Francisco respectively. It was fitting that while this announcement was being made, Milwaukee, the original gypsy, was winning its first World Series. As their jilted fans howled, pudgy Warren Giles, the National League president, snorted, "Who needs New York anyway?"

And George V. McLaughlin vowed never to speak to Walter O'Malley again. Despite O'Malley's attempts to heal the breach, he never did.

By this time, New York Mayor Robert F. Wagner realized that loss of the two major-league baseball teams had become a political liability. Rightly or wrongly, he was being blamed for their departure because of his failure to come up with a stadium site satisfactory to O'Malley. A month after the ball club's shocking move, Wagner made a phone call to Bill Shea's midtown Manhattan law office. The two men were personal friends and political allies. Shea was talking to a client when Wagner's call came through.

"Bill," Wagner said without preamble, "I'm appointing a committee to bring National League baseball back to New York. Jim Farley's on it, and Bernard Gimbel, and Clint Blume. And, Bill, I want you to be the chairman. You're the only one who can put it over."

Shea, who felt the committee was long overdue, accepted with one proviso, that his chairmanship should come from fellow committee members, not the Mayor. This was done.

Farley, the former Postmaster General, still had powerful political connections in Washington. These would come in handy. Gimbel was one of the city's leading merchants. Blume, who once pitched briefly for the Giants, was president of the Real Estate Board of New York. It was a powerful team.

During this time, the Cleveland Indians were putting together their minor-league teams. A young pitcher was advanced from Class D to Class C. It would be two years before Ron Taylor earned another promotion.

Wagner knew what he was doing when he proposed the dynamic fifty-year-old Shea as workhorse of the committee. Shea was a native New Yorker, profane, earthy, able, energetic, and ambitious. He aspired to no elected position himself, although he might have been a natural. With his Irish charm, he could talk like the man in the street while outsmarting Wall Streeters before breakfast.

Shea could wheel as well as deal. He had spent most of his early childhood in Brooklyn before moving back to his native borough of Manhattan, where he played basketball and was elected student-body president at George Washington High. After he finished high school and enrolled at New York University, he thought it was a shame for graduation to break up that old high school basketball gang. And that's how Fort Washington Prep was chartered. Shea and his old high school teammates, representing this fictitious academy, ran roughshod over all scholastic competition that winter before making a fatal mistake. They entered a Pennsylvania high school tournament where a referee from New York recognized them. That was the end of $25 guarantee checks for each game, and Fort Washington Prep closed its doors before it could graduate a single student.

Shea had enrolled at NYU on a basketball scholarship and also played football and lacrosse as a freshman. But by then the husky 6-footer had decided to become a lawyer, and this ambition created a problem. It took six years of college to become a lawyer, and Shea's NYU scholarship covered only four. The answer was simplicity itself. Shea just transferred to Georgetown in Washington, D.C., where he would have three years of athletic eligibility and scholarship time remaining *after* sitting out one season as a transfer. Although he went to Georgetown on a football grant, Shea later switched to basketball.

On graduation from Georgetown in 1931, Shea joined the law firm that handled the Brooklyn Trust Company's affairs. There he met George V. McLaughlin.

At first Shea thought it would be a simple matter to bring the National League back to New York. He would catalogue the city's many virtues, repeat Mayor Wagner's promise to build a municipal stadium in Flushing Meadow, and then sit back to wait for volunteers from baseball's several marginal franchises. When no volunteers were forthcoming, Shea became the aggressor. He contacted the Cincinnati Reds, the Pittsburgh Pirates, and the Philadelphia Phillies, coming closer to landing the first two. All had plenty of incentive to move but one compelling reason to stay: their owners were rooted in the respective cities. "I realized then what a terrible thing I was trying to do," Shea said later. "I was trying to swipe a team from those cities just the way it had been done to us."

Shea then proceeded with his second plan to get New York back in the National League. He would persuade baseball to expand and put a new team in New York. Everybody in baseball agreed this was a splendid idea. And nobody in baseball did anything about it. After all, it took two to dance the expansion tango. New York would have to come in with a new partner to make a ten-team league. "Now where would we get that tenth city?" they asked sadly.

It didn't take long for the New York group to realize that the National League felt absolutely no obligation to the city that had supported two of its teams for so many years. In fact, the group began to suspect that there was a secret deal to keep them out of the National League entirely. In return for free rights to the West Coast territory, the Nationals apparently had given the American League, meaning the Yankees, New York City as their private fief. No wonder Shea was to feel later that the Yankees "were constantly sticking knives in us."

That winter of 1958, Shea tried to stir things up with an open threat to start his own league, but Giles responded by announcing, "Right now New York is a dead issue in the National League."

This same winter, a slender New Yorker was completing his three-year hitch at the Norfolk, Virginia, Naval Air Station. Ignored by the pros when he finished high school, he looked good enough playing service ball for the Chicago White Sox to sign twenty-one-year-old Al Weis for one of their Class-D farm clubs.

At this point, George V. McLaughlin entered the picture again. Why didn't Bill Shea get in touch with Branch Rickey, an old man of seventy-seven, but still alert and possessing the most fertile mind in baseball. Some might claim that competition for this particular accolade wasn't the greatest, but Rickey would have been an intellectual giant in any company. Rickey, McLaughlin pointed out, had some interesting ideas about forming a third major league. He and McLaughlin had gotten to know one another when the Mahatma—

as Rickey was called—was running the Dodgers before he was forced out of Brooklyn by our old friend Walter O'Malley.

Rickey had maintained for years that baseball expansion was inevitable but it would be foolish for the established leagues to do this by adding new teams. Competition is the keystone of fan interest, and the new teams would not be competitive for years. (How right he was!) The answer, according to this bushy-browed baseball genius, was the establishment of a third league. All eight new teams would be of equal ability, so there would be real competition while they were achieving parity with the older clubs.

Out of meetings between Shea and Rickey was born the Continental League, a confederation that never played a game but still had a profound effect on the course of all professional sports in the following decade. As the new league began to take shape, organized baseball continued to play its little game. "We would welcome the application of a third league," Commissioner Frick declared piously in the spring of 1959 while Shea was crisscrossing the continent seeking backers for the new teams.

Shea's first job, of course, was to establish the New York entry. For one thing, this had been his original assignment from Mayor Wagner. For another, any league had to have a strong New York outlet in order to be considered major.

Shea's initial contact in building a New York franchise was with Dwight F. (Pete) Davis, Jr., the wealthy and convivial son of the donor of the famous Davis Cup in tennis. Davis was a dedicated baseball fan who would travel from coast to coast to see important games in a close pennant race. He felt that a perfect person to join, and possibly head, the New York syndicate was Mrs. Charles Shipman (Joan) Payson, who, with her brother, John Hay (Jock) Whitney, shared the fabulous Whitney fortune. Mrs. Payson and her brother owned the famous Greentree Stable, but she was just as interested in baseball as in racing. In fact, just before the team left New York she had been persuaded to buy a share of stock in the Giants by her financial adviser, M. Donald Grant. Her mother also had been a fanatic Giant fan, and Mrs. Payson had been desolated when the team left town.

Shea knew of Mrs. Payson as a fan and agreed with Davis as to her suitability. She certainly had the interest and the financial resources, plus the identification as a bona fide New Yorker. It didn't hurt either that her brother was publisher of the New York *Herald-*

Tribune. Shea knew he would need all the editorial support he could get in his fight for a stadium and a new league. Davis, who knew Mrs. Payson, made the introductions, and they all met for the first time in Shea's law office. Grant was along, too.

After the meeting, they repaired for cocktails to the nearby Biltmore Hotel. Like Shea, Mrs. Payson would have preferred to buy an established team and move it to New York. Although receptive to the idea of a new league, she still was not convinced, and it took several meetings with the eloquent Branch Rickey finally to persuade her to join the venture. Later, when asked why she had put up some $3 million to launch the Mets with herself as major stockholder, she would reply, "Whatever would not make me buy them? Wouldn't anybody if they had the chance?"

After enrolling Davis and Mrs. Payson, Shea added a third major backer. The final portion of what would be three equal shares went to Mrs. Dorothy Killam of Montreal, a wealthy widow who also had tried to keep the National League in New York by attempting to buy the Dodgers. Mrs. Killam, originally from St. Louis, was a forceful woman who liked to boast that she had been able to double the $100 million estate left by her late husband, who had made his money in Canadian mining. Mrs. Killam once spent $80,000 for an open telephone line to Toronto so she could hear the full radio account of the 1947 Yankee-Dodger World Series while she was confined by illness. Only a real Dodger fan would have pulled a stunt like that. Mrs. Killam had been recommended to Shea by one of his clients, Canadian millionaire Jack Kent Cooke. Cooke was backing the Continental League's Toronto franchise.

Others in the New York syndicate with lesser interests were Grant, G. Herbert Walker, son of the donor of golf's Walker Cup, and William Simpson, president of a travel agency. Grant, a stockbroker, had been the only member of the Giants' board of directors to vote against the team's shift to San Francisco. "I still vote no," he thundered at a press conference introducing the syndicate that spring. More than a bit of a stuffed shirt, Grant, a native of Montreal and the son of a Hall of Fame hockey player, jealously guarded Mrs. Payson's interests as well as his position at the right hand of this bouyant but almost childlike and shy millionairess, who enjoyed more than anything, except for her children and grandchildren, a ninth-inning rally, a photo finish, and a sing-along around the piano.

Mrs. Charles Shipman Payson christens them "The Mets"
with a baseball bat as M. Donald Grant
holds a bottle of champagne in his glove.

(Other sports held no real fascination for her. When the New York Titans, later to become the Jets, went bankrupt, there were reports that she would buy them out to provide a winter tenant for Shea Stadium. "What an appalling suggestion," she intoned regally, sounding for all the world as if someone had just proposed that she wear a pants suit to the opera.)

This large group of owners, of course, could not survive in harmony. Mrs. Killam dropped out early when her demand to be named president was vetoed. At that time, Shea was fighting for legislative approval of a new municipal stadium. The president of this new team had to be a New Yorker, otherwise the proposal was doomed. Mrs. Payson bought Mrs. Killam's interest and eventually those of Davis and Simpson when they were forced out later on. That left Mrs. Payson in control of 80 percent of the stock, with Grant and Walker sharing the rest.

By midsummer, Shea felt confident enough to announce four more cities as founding franchises and to give the new confederation its name, the Continental League. Joining New York were Toronto, Houston, Denver, and Minneapolis–St. Paul. Eventually, in order, Atlanta, Dallas–Fort Worth, and Buffalo enlisted, to complete an eight-team circuit. Branch Rickey was named league president, and an application was submitted for acceptance by organized baseball.

The Continentals were greeted with open arms by the establishment. Unfortunately, at the end of those open arms were hands clutching knives. "We'll be glad to have you if you meet the ten requirements for a third major league that we set earlier," baseball crooned confidently. They knew those terms were impossible.

Included in the requirements were unspecified indemnity payments to the minor leagues whose towns they were taking over, even though in many cases the franchise operators would be unchanged. As soon as they received the indemnity demands, the Continentals knew just how welcome they were in baseball's little club. In 1954, the St. Louis Browns had paid the International League less than $50,000 to move into Baltimore. Five years later, the near-bankrupt minor leagues were demanding several million from the new boys. Talk about inflation! American League hints of expansion into a couple of Continental cities and the imposition of unrealistic deadlines persuaded the new league to repeat its earlier threats to operate outside baseball's structure if necessary.

The late Senator Estes Kefauver, chairman of the Senate's antitrust subcommittee, had been planning for some time to investigate baseball. However, Shea and the Continentals had persuaded him to hold off as long as it seemed they could get a piece of the monopoly action. But now the Continentals pressed for legislation only to find that baseball was pushing its own new law, one that would exempt it from existing antitrust statutes. Baseball's bill, which would have killed the Continentals by enabling baseball to lock up all the talent, almost slipped through both houses of Congress in late 1959. But in the last of the ninth, Farley and Shea received an urgent phone call from a close friend who was counsel to one of the interested committees. "You'd better get down here in a hurry —you're getting clobbered," they were told.

The Continentals may have been neophytes in baseball, but they were .300 hitters in the political big leagues. The owner of the Cons' Denver club was Bob Howsam, whose father-in-law was Edwin Johnson, a former senator and governor of Colorado and once president of baseball's Western League. Johnson, still a political power in his state, used his influence with one of Colorado's senators to keep organized baseball's winning run pinned on third while the Continentals got their turn at bat. This was the critical power play. Both bills were voted down, but the real defeat was suffered by baseball, which got a look at the new league's legislative muscle. These crucial votes, more important than any late-season game between pennant contenders, were taken in June of 1960.

Meanwhile, on April 29, 1960, the city of New York voted to authorize construction of a new stadium in Flushing Meadow, site of the 1939 World's Fair. They said it would be ready in 1962. They proved to be two years off but still well ahead of the schedule provided by those who said it would never be done.

> About the time the city's Board of Estimate was voting, eighteen-year-old Art Shamsky came to bat for the first time as a professional and hit a home run for Cincinnati's Class-D farm team in Geneva, New York. During the battle in Congress, Don Cardwell pitched a no-hitter for the Chicago Cubs against St. Louis.

While waiting for its new park, the proposed Continental baseball team would play in the ancient Polo Grounds, which had been rescued just in time from being razed for an apartment development, the fate of Brooklyn's Ebbets Field. A team in the new American Football League, scheduled to start play that fall, also would debut in the Polo Grounds and then move to Flushing Meadow. Few would guess that in 1969 the new stadium would fly the world-championship banners for both its tenants. (The Continental League also had a great effect on the course of pro football. There would have been no New York team in the AFL without the promise of a new stadium and thus, of course, no real stature for the new league. Also, in many cases there were close connections and even overlapping of owners in both circuits. It is one of Shea's dubious honors that he introduced Lamar Hunt, founder of the AFL, to Harry Wismer, who would run the new league's New York franchise into bankruptcy and almost wreck the whole endeavor.)

Stymied in Congress, the baseball establishment finally gave in. On the first of August, 1960, leaders of the Continental League were summoned to Chicago. The Cons had hopes of being accepted as a unit, but baseball wasn't that generous. If the new league agreed to fold, four of its members were promised acceptance in an expansion of the existing leagues to ten teams each by 1961 or 1962. It was assumed that the new franchises would go to New York, Toronto, Houston, and Minneapolis–St. Paul.*

Soon after the 1960 Pirate-Yankee World Series, the expansion committees of the two leagues met. Still fearing that shiv in the back, Shea called Mayor Wagner late at night before the National League meeting in Chicago's Sheraton-Blackstone Hotel and persuaded him to wire all the concerned owners repeating his pledge to build a stadium. Shea wanted to give the Nationals no excuses to back down, and on October 17, "with unanimous enthusiasm," the National League granted franchises to New York and Houston effective 1962. The meeting was presided over by Warren C. Giles of "Who needs New York?" fame. Walter O'Malley offered the motion. That was a real nice touch.

The American League still had to hold *its* meeting, however, and this group's actions nine days later in New York's Savoy-Hilton Hotel lived up to neither the letter nor the spirit of what the Continentals thought they had been granted. In an unscheduled if not unexpected move, the Americans voted to allow Calvin Griffith to shift his Senators and his relative-laden payroll from Washington to Minneapolis–St. Paul. They then placed expansion teams in Washington and in O'Malley's once-private duchy of Los Angeles. All three moves were to become effective in 1961, a year before the Nationals went to ten teams.

---

* How the Outs assume all the attitudes of the Ins once they are accepted by the establishment is an interesting study in human nature. For Houston to be taken into the National League, Dallas–Fort Worth, among others, had to postpone its own major-league dreams. Yet, less than ten years later, when Dallas–Fort Worth had a chance to get a big-league franchise, it was Houston and its O'Malley of a president, Judge Roy Hofheinz, who vetoed its selection.

No matter how you slice it, the Cons had been conned again, getting three, not four, of their cities accepted into the majors and only two sets of their owners. But who could protest? The new league's firm eight-team front had been broken and the Continental League standard-bearers in Minnesota could hardly complain. After all, their stated aim had been to bring big-league baseball to the Twin Cities, and now their neighbors had a chance to see not a faltering expansion team but a real pennant contender. The people who really got creamed on this exchange were long-suffering Washington fans. Just as soon as their perennial losers got good, they left town, and the Senators—at least Griffith left the old name—had to start over.

Perhaps the most interesting sidelight of all, though, was the haste with which the American League rushed into Los Angeles once the Yankees' monopoly in New York was about to be ended. Anybody who still called baseball a game and not a business probably still wrote letters to Santa Claus. New Yorkers at this point were not inclined to argue the fine points. Shea had done his job for the city, and when baseball entered a second round of expansion less than a decade later, all those new franchise holders also owed a debt to the forceful attorney. Shea had rocked the boat—at considerable personal expense plus the neglect of his law practice, his family, and his golf game—and the unforgiving establishment would never be the same. But in his fight Shea had made more than enough friends where he wanted to have them, in his hometown. When the new stadium finally opened in Flushing Meadow, there was no argument over its name.

As William A. Shea Municipal Stadium was dedicated on April 16, 1964, Shea declared, "I feel highly honored that Mayor Wagner and members of the City Council have seen fit to put my name on this wonderful structure. Now I just hope I live long enough to see a World Series played here."

3

The Odd Couple

A pebble, one crummy pebble. Who knows which direction the Mets would have taken if only there had been a decent infield in Pittsburgh?

Four days before New York was officially welcomed back to the National League, the Yankees and Pirates were playing the seventh and deciding game of the 1960 World Series in Pittsburgh. The date was October 13, and the score in the eighth inning was 7-4 in favor of the Yankees.

The Pirates had two more tries to catch up, and Gino Cimoli led off the inning with a single. Then Bill Virdon, a former Yankee, followed with a simple grounder toward shortstop Tony Kubek. Double play, threat over, only four more outs between the Yankees and another world championship. But the ground ball hit that pebble, took a sharp hop, and struck Kubek in the Adam's apple. Both runners were safe, and the inspired Pirates rallied for five runs and a 9-7 lead.

The Yankees managed to tie in the top of the ninth, but Bill Mazeroski led off the last inning for the Pirates and hit Ralph Terry's second pitch, a high fast ball, over the fence for a home run. Mazeroski's blow won the game and the series for Pittsburgh.

Mazeroski's homer—and that little pebble—were to have a profound effect on the still-embryonic Mets. Casey Stengel was manager of the Yankees, and he was seventy years old. George M. Weiss was their general manager and he was sixty-six. Dan Topping and Del Webb were the owners, and their ages are immaterial. What is important is that they seized on this World Series loss as an excuse to fire both Stengel and Weiss.

Oh, they didn't blame it on that pebble. In that case somebody would have had to fire the Pittsburgh groundskeeper. They just said they were instituting a mandatory sixty-five-year-old retirement policy and that would include Stengel and Weiss. Voluntary retirement, Topping and Webb chorused, and Stengel even went along with them in the preliminary announcements. But when he sat down at the formal press conference and warmed himself with a couple of bourbons, Casey admitted simply, "I was discharged."

Two factors were behind this ruthless severance, not the first or the last by Topping and Webb. Topping was fairly active in the day-to-day activities of the team, and the millionaire playboy thought highly of one of Stengel's coaches, Ralph Houk. Houk had already turned down several managerial offers, but if he didn't get the Yankee job now, he might be lost to the organization. Weiss and Stengel had been friends for decades. As long as he was in charge, Weiss would not stand for his old colleague's being fired.

More to the point, though, was the matter of attendance. Topping and Webb saw the Yankees as a money machine and eventually milked it dry before selling out to the Columbia Broadcasting System. When the Giants and the Dodgers left town, the Yankees thought this would usher in an era of unparalleled prosperity. Instead, attendance in 1958 dropped by almost 70,000 to the lowest figure in fifteen years, even though the Yankees won another world championship. There were improvements in 1959 and 1960 but nothing startling. With the new Mets looming over the horizon, Topping and Webb thought they had to give their team, which had won ten pennants and seven world championships in twelve years under Stengel, a new and youthful image. (What irony that this action provided the Mets with their greatest gate attraction!) On October 18—the day after the Mets officially were born and only five days after Tony Kubek received his celebrated pain in the neck—the Yankees fired Stengel. Two weeks later Weiss followed him into exile.

Stengel went back to the West Coast, to his home in Glendale, California, where he was vice president of a bank. After all these years of traveling, his wife, Edna, who had met him when he played outfield for the Giants in 1923, was glad to have him home. Weiss lived in Greenwich, Connecticut, a suburb of New York. He

The starting team: George Weiss (left) and Casey Stengel.

chafed at the idea of retirement. So did his wife, Hazel. "I married him for better or for worse, but not for lunch," she complained to friends with a smile.

There were chances for Stengel to manage elsewhere, none of them compelling. So he went to his bank, worked on his autobiography, and kept his hand in baseball by helping advise the owners of the new Los Angeles team in the American League, who had to rush into operation that spring.

One of the Angels' picks in the December expansion draft was a Brooklyn-born infielder from the Tigers. Eddie Yost would play into the following season and then become a coach.

Weiss also received many calls through the winter. In all, there were six offers to run a ball club, but all involved moving away from the New York area and giving up his home. Weiss, acting with characteristic caution, elected to wait until spring to make up his mind. Well off, as was Stengel, and, like Casey, still receiving deferred salary payments from the Yankees, he was in no hurry.

The day before Weiss was due to drive down to Florida—the spring training habit was hard to break—he received a phone call from M. Donald Grant. "Have you made any plans?" Grant asked. "If not, we'd be interested in talking with you about joining the Mets." Weiss told Grant he was still uncommitted and drove into the city that night to meet with him. They parted with a promise to talk again in Florida, and one day Weiss flew from Clearwater, where he was staying, to Hobe Sound on the east coast, where Mrs. Payson had a winter home. (He had known both Mrs. Payson and Grant casually before this.) Tentative agreement was reached, depending on whether the Mets could sort out some ownership problems. Jack Kent Cooke of Toronto, who had been left out when the Continental League folded, wanted to buy into the Mets. If this could be arranged, there was an understanding that Branch Rickey would become their chief executive officer.

When Cooke's inclusion in the syndicate could not be worked out, the way was clear for Weiss. Agreement was quickly reached. Because the terms of his severance from the Yankees prevented him from assuming another general manager's job, Weiss was named "president" of the new team. An announcement to that effect was made on March 14, 1961, in the Shamrock Isle Hotel in Miami Beach by the Metropolitan Baseball Club, Inc.

On May 8 in New York, Mrs. Payson formally christened her team the Mets by breaking a bottle of champagne on a baseball bat. She had chosen the name herself. It seemed to have a nice ring.

> *On the last day of that month, the Chicago Cubs would sign a junior-college All-American out of Campbell College in North Carolina. They started Cal Koonce off in pretty fast company, Class B. In mid-June, the Cleveland Indians gave $65,000 in bonus money to a football and baseball star at Grambling College. Tommie Agee had to spend his first season in Class D.*

Weiss knew his team wouldn't be operating for another season, so he set to work building an organization. He swept out many employees who had been hired by the old Continental League apparatus and named as his chief scout a former Red Sox executive who had once pitched for the Yankees, Johnny Murphy. As the 1961 season unfolded, Weiss and Murphy had scouts watching pro baseball players in every classification. They knew they would be at the mercy of the established teams' expansion draft lists. They had to be sure they picked the best players available, no matter in what low minor league they toiled.

All through this period, of course, Weiss was thinking about a field manager. His list of leading candidates consisted of one name: Casey Stengel. If Weiss had accepted one of the other six offers he had received, Stengel still would have been his man. Weiss and Stengel had been friends since crossing paths in the Eastern League in 1925. Casey had just ended his major-league career and was playing manager at Worcester, Massachusetts. Weiss owned a rival franchise in New Haven, Connecticut.

Weiss joined the Yankee organization as farm director in 1932 and was advanced to the post of general manager after the 1947 season. At his first opportunity, following the 1948 campaign, Weiss brought Stengel back from Oakland to be his manager. Casey had managed in the majors before, never with any success. But Weiss knew the great baseball mind his old friend possessed, and he ignored considerable criticism to bring Stengel East. The record proves this to be one of his most astute moves. (The other was when he recommended in 1935 that the Yankees complete an expensive deal with San Francisco for a sore-kneed outfielder named Joe DiMaggio.) Weiss called Stengel almost immediately after he signed with the Mets, but Casey vacillated. From the beginning, Stengel nursed a hunger to manage, but he didn't like the idea of leaving his California home to resume living eight months a year in hotel rooms.

Finally, though, the 1961 season was drawing to a close. "I've got to have a manager before the draft," Weiss pleaded.

"Give me a little more time," Stengel hedged.

But one day the phone rang in Casey's Glendale home. It was Mrs. Payson. "Casey, we need you to manage our team," she said. Never immune to flattery, Stengel responded to her plea. Besides, if he ever managed again, New York was the place to be. With the Mets, he could really stick it to that other team across the river, the one that had said he was too old. Baseball had been good to him, now he could repay the favor.

If ever there was an "odd couple" in baseball, it was Stengel and Weiss. Perhaps that's why they worked together so well. Casey was a public man, outspoken, egocentric, colorful, witty, eager to take a chance, an innovator and a showman. Weiss, on the other hand, was shy, conservative, and devious, a private man whom columnist Jimmy Cannon had dubbed "Lonesome George." Stengel loved to match wits with the press and always won. Weiss feared and mistrusted any writer he hadn't met before 1930. With his right hand tucked reassuringly in his coat pocket, the portly Weiss would duck his head like a teen-ager when talking to any but his closest friends. "He'd give you hell for a $5 or $10 mistake, but tell you to forget about it if you made a mistake for $5,000," an old associate once said. Many long-time Weiss aides would testify to his kindness, but he struck terror in most of his employees and few got a chance to make more than a couple of those four-figure mistakes.

Baseball's winter meetings usually are open season for job hunting as well as player trades. One former Weiss aide recalls how George waited until the last day of the meetings to fire him. Weiss thus got maximum benefit from the man before cutting him off too late to get another job.

Most organizations reflect the man on the top. For years the Yankees mirrored Weiss, cold, impersonal, aloof, and efficient. Stengel was merely a colorful adjunct. With the Mets, though, Stengel was their leading figure from the beginning, and for years they reflected his personality even though they existed as the creature of Weiss.

It was Weiss who set the pattern for the Mets in the expansion draft, going almost completely for veterans who would draw fans in competition with the Yankees. However, even after he was proved wrong, he refused to concede and tear up his team. The way the Mets were accepted by New York fans, he could have played anybody. The heroes were not the old names but the new— Rod Kanehl, Marv Throneberry, Choo-Choo Coleman, and, later, Ron Swoboda. The old names were the millstones, and yet Weiss fought discarding them. And when he did, he brought in more, the Duke Sniders and Warren Spahns. Mainly, Weiss, an American Leaguer for thirty years, misjudged the hold the National League still had on New Yorkers. He didn't need familiar retreads like Gus Bell to draw fans. Stan Musial, Willie Mays, and Sandy Koufax, all returning to New York for the first time in five years, would take care of that.

Additionally, Weiss kept his eyes on the ledger. He tried to show a book profit on every player he discarded. How could you simply release a player who had cost you $75,000? You had to get something back.

Weiss also brought his old Yankee tactics over to the Mets. With the powerful, all-winning Bronx Bombers, Weiss would sit in his hotel suite during baseball meetings and await petitioners begging to deal for his surplus talent. After he took over the Mets he continued to sit and wait. Only nobody came. When he did get close to a deal, he often ruined it at the last minute by asking for just a little bit more.

Weiss also hesitated to get into the bonus field while it was still wide open. Throwing large sums of money at untried youngsters was repulsive to this son of a New Haven grocer, and his refusal to enter bonus competition for top prospects directly led to the eventual decline of the Yankees. Weiss's successors are still paying that price.

As close as they were and as much as they respected each other, Weiss and Stengel disagreed often over young players. Stengel was always willing to take a chance. He'd just as soon get rid of a ball player who'd never been any good. "At least this young feller has never failed," he'd say. "As for the other feller, I seen what he done."

In all of his financial conservatism, Weiss had a full ally in Grant, Mrs. Payson's man. Neither Grant nor Weiss ever grasped the full meaning of the Mets. Weiss, in fact, appeared embarrassed by the appeal of what to him was just a lousy ball club. And he and Grant both attempted that first year to have the famous banners banned from the ball park. (During the long years of frustration, a fan once showed up late in the season with a sign reading "Welcome to Grant's Tomb." It was confiscated. Even after banners became part of the Met folklore and were recognized by an annual competition, uncomplimentary references to the Met management were carefully screened out.)

Both Grant and Weiss were primarily money men. The ledger was proof of their success in running the Mets for Mrs. Payson. The tragedy was that Mrs. Payson would have spent any number of her millions to have achieved early respectability on the field. By counting only profit and loss, they did her no real service.

Years later, Weiss would look back at the Mets' futile beginnings. "I still disagree with people who poke fun at the first Mets' ball club," he said. "It was not a bad club from the standpoint of names . . . and we drew a million people."

Weiss still missed the point. And when he walked into the hysterical Met clubhouse after the World Series was won and saw women on the premises, his first thought was, "This isn't like the old Yankees at all."

The thread of comparison with the old Yankees was established in the very beginning when, on October 2, 1961, Weiss was able to announce officially that Casey Stengel would be their first manager. This would not be the last time the Mets would score on a Yankee error.

Three days later Cincinnati beat Ralph Houk's Yankees, 6-2, in the second game of the World Series. The Yankee runs came on a homer by Yogi Berra, the last World Series home run of his long career. This was the only game the Reds would win in the Series, and their go-ahead run was scored on the daring base-running of infielder Elio Chacon.

The day after Yogi's home run, the Mets signed a thirty-year lease with the city for use of the still-unfinished Shea Stadium. On October 10, the day after the Series ended, the Mets and Houston were given a look at the list of players available in the expansion draft. They almost threw up. The National League had done it to them again. The list consisted almost entirely of has-beens and never-woulds, the injury-prone and the malcontents. It was no coincidence that when the Mets finished drafting they had something like half a dozen player-representatives on their roster.

There had been some criticism of the way the American League had rushed into expansion the year before, but this precipitate move actually helped the new teams. Rosters were frozen on the spot, leaving some pretty fair players exposed. The Nationals, however, were forewarned and used the year to cover up all their good prospects. If any good players were still available, it was a mistake. Houston's general manager, Paul Richards, publicly threatened to withdraw from the whole business when he saw the list of culls and misfits. Weiss and the Mets were just as angry but realistically knew they had gone too far to pull back. "But I was pretty chagrined when I saw that list," Weiss admitted later.

Both new teams entered the expansion draft with an over-all

strategy. Houston figured its fans would be happy to see major-league ball of any caliber. There was no competition within many hundreds of miles. The Colts would go for younger players and, since they would play for a couple of years in a temporary stadium with deep fences and bad lights, they would concentrate on pitching and defense.

Weiss, starting with the assumption there were no outstanding young prospects available, went in the opposite direction. Since he was seeking fans from a sophisticated audience in competition with the Yankees, he felt he had to go for names, no matter how old and halt the bodies belonging to those names might be. Also, since the Mets would be playing at least their first season in the Polo Grounds, a home-run paradise, he went for elephant-legged sluggers.

The reasoning wasn't bad, but the Mets, as it turned out, were.

The selection process took four hours at the Netherland-Hilton Hotel in Cincinnati. The first player tabbed was infielder Eddie Bressoud (later to be a Met) by Houston. The Mets opened by taking catcher Hobie Landrith and followed Houston's selection of Bob Aspromonte by grabbing one of their all-time heroes, Elio Chacon.

All told, the Mets took twenty-two men for $1,800,000. The Colts picked twenty-three for $1,850,000. The price was outrageous for the talent it bought, but not so bad considering it actually was a franchise fee. Besides, giving these players inflated book values helped the new clubs on tax depreciation. (Yes, teams in all sports are allowed to depreciate their ball players just as if they were tractors or typewriters.) Under the drafting procedure, each team could pick four players from a premium group at $125,000 apiece, sixteen more from another list at $75,000 apiece, and an unlimited number of special "bargains" at $50,000 each. That last list was so appealing the Mets took only two, including Jim Hickman, while the Colts grabbed three.

Gil Hodges went for $75,000, and the Mets' four premium choices were pitchers Jay Hook of Cincinnati and Bob Miller of St. Louis, infielder Don Zimmer of Chicago, and outfielder Lee Walls of Philadelphia.*

Before the season opened, Walls was sent with $100,000 in cash to the Dodgers for infielder Charlie Neal, outfielder Richie Ash-

* The complete list of original Met draftees appears on pages 182–183.

burn was purchased from the Cubs, and outfielder Frank Thomas was obtained for cash and a player from the Braves. Half a dozen other journeymen also were purchased from big-league teams to fill out the roster. Only when most of these players were returned to their original clubs late in spring training was it learned that many of these purchases were on a conditional basis. Many of the players, who had thought they were competing even-up for positions with the Mets, were crushed on learning the hard way that they had just been brought in for a tryout. And writers covering the club quickly discovered they had to look for the fine print themselves whenever informing fans about another Weiss "deal."

But all that winter hopes remained high. The Mets played the role of name-droppers throughout the off-season. Gil Hodges, Jay Hook, Roger Craig, Elio Chacon, Felix Mantilla, Gus Bell, Frank Thomas, Richie Ashburn, Don Zimmer, Hobie Landrith, Charlie Neal, and even Ed Bouchee were recognizable major-leaguers. The Mets played them up for all they were worth. More than they were worth, as it turned out.

A young magazine writer in New York was so impressed by this lineup that he even wrote an article promising "The Mets Won't Finish Last." He didn't have to feel too bad. Almost until the day the Mets started playing games that counted, everybody agreed with him.

The Frauds

Maybe the gods that look after drunks and kids who play stickball in city streets were trying to tell them something. Here it was the day before they were supposed to open their first training camp and the Mets' uniforms still hadn't arrived in Saint Petersburg, Florida. Herb Norman, the equipment manager, sat up like an expectant father. Finally, at 2:00 A.M., he got the delivery, brand-new gray road uniforms with "New York" lettered across the front of the jerseys. Naturally, the order was fouled up. The smallest-sized pants were 34s. Al Jackson, the teeny left-hander, so light he often wasn't even able to activate those automatic doors at supermarkets, looked as if he were wearing a tent. But he didn't complain. He had spent seven seasons pitching minor-league ball for the Pirates. For a chance in the majors, he'd pitch in his drawers. Jay Hook, a bona fide major-leaguer, had reported to camp early. He used his old Cincinnati uniform.

Casey Stengel, who had spent his last managerial years in the American League, recognized few of his new players. But one he acknowledged was his long-time World Series adversary, Gil Hodges. Hodges was famous for his skill at leaning off first base, the quicker to meet the throw from his infielders. When he did this, his foot would leave the bag, but he was seldom caught. This split second saved the Dodgers many an out. "I'm glad to have you on my side 'cause you're the biggest cheater," Stengel said. Stengel liked anybody who was slick. Gil was flattered.

At least at the beginning there was some life to the Mets.
Charging onto the field at the Polo Grounds for their first workout are
(from left) Frank Thomas, Gil Hodges, Don Zimmer, and Roger Craig.

After opening remarks from the manager, the players donned
their warmup jackets and headed out on the field. It was a raw
day, the kind of day that frequently leads Maury Allen, veteran
baseball writer of the New York *Post* to proclaim, "Florida is a
fraud." But there was a crowd in the stands. Saint Petersburg is a
retirement city. It reeks of old age and social security. The retirees
rise late and go to bed early so they can manage on two meals a
day. Their favorite pastime is watching the traffic from sidewalk
benches. The Yankees had recently deserted Saint Petersburg for
Fort Lauderdale of Florida's east coast. Now George Weiss was
filling that void and the old-timers had something free to occupy
their afternoons. They especially enjoyed watching seventy-one-

year-old Casey Stengel make a lie of their arthritic old age. He always got the biggest hand. "Well, those people are elderly and I got a few wrinkles in my face," he explained.

Then he took his players on a tour of the diamond. "You can make a living here," he told this collection of retreads and rejects. (It was five more days before the home uniforms arrived. Only then did "Mets" take the field.)

Hodges was acknowledged as senior of the new players, and Norman assigned him the No. 1 locker closest to the training room. Veterans with big-league credentials were grouped around him. Rookies were shoved against the east wall farthest from the playing field.

"Someday I'll make that west wall," vowed one rookie who was quick to catch on to the social stratification...and he did. His name was Rod Kanehl and he had spent eight seasons in the minor leagues. The Yankees had owned him, but some summers they didn't even think he was worth keeping in their farm system. They'd

Rod Kanehl didn't have much finesse around second base,
but he'd stand his ground to make the double play.
Walt Bond of Houston is the runner.

lend him out to another organization. But when the Yankees two years before had offered him a job as playing manager in the lower minors, he turned it down for one last shot at the bigs. Expansion got it for him.

Once, of course, he had been a prospect. He even attended an early Yankee training camp for future stars, and this is what finally got him a job with the Mets. In one intrasquad game he had to range deep after a fly ball and he hurdled a fence to get it. (He'd gone to college on a track scholarship. His father was the track coach.) Casey Stengel never forgot that play, probably because Casey Stengel never forgets anything. When he saw that winter that Kanehl was available, he demanded that George Weiss bring him to camp. For the next three years, Kanehl was the embodiment of all that was good in the Mets. He was a blithe spirit who loved life, and it seemed to be a shame to end each glorious day by going to bed. A native of St. Louis, he explored New York by subway. He and his red-haired wife and their boys made life with the Mets an adventure.

Kanehl could do a lot of little things on a baseball field, and he did them with verve if not with skill. The first banner in the Polo Grounds was dedicated to Hot Rod. Stengel once offered a bonus of $50 to any player who would let himself get hit with a pitched ball to force in a run when the bases were loaded. Kanehl was the only Met to collect. Before he left, he had played every position but pitcher and catcher. During the period when he had to fill in at second base, the Mets made more double plays than at any time in their first season. Kanehl's problem was that he never mastered the technique of avoiding the sliding runner. So he took a steady diet of spikes in the shins and got the double plays.* Weiss fought Stengel's efforts to keep Kanehl around. When he got the chance, Weiss shipped Rod to the minors and slashed his salary 50 percent so he'd be forced to leave baseball. A shame.

The original Met roster was loaded with former Dodgers, and Norman tried to keep them all together. There were Hodges, Roger Craig, Charlie Neal, Don Zimmer, and Clem Labine in that group and more to come. The Dodgers had tradition and meaning for New York's National League fans, plus an aura of respectability, since they had been winning pennants rather regularly in Los An-

---

* Rod Kanehl also did the world's best Casey Stengel imitation. Whitey Herzog, later a Met coach who went straight and took a front office job, was No. 2. Herzog had known Stengel briefly as a Yankee.

geles. The tradition was nice, but, in effect, the massing of these former Dodgers was to set up the first of many cliques that kept the Mets from becoming a team. Only when Hodges returned as manager was this divisiveness ended.

Once the Mets began playing exhibition games, the cracks began to show, at least to Stengel. He called one of his players "a lower intestine" and another was "my road apple left-hander." To fans he'd trumpet, "Come on out and see the amazin' Mets," but to intimates he would confess, "This team is a fraud."

Those frauds could be cranked up once in a while, though, and on March 22, the Yankees came to Saint Petersburg for an exhibition game. This would be the first confrontation between Stengel and the team that had fired him. "I got along without [Dan] Topping before I managed the Yankees and I'm getting along without him now that I'm managing the Mets. As far as this game is concerned, it really doesn't matter," Stengel growled.

He was lying, of course.

The Mets' best pitchers, Roger Craig and Al Jackson, were tuned up to go against the Yankees, and so were the rest of the regulars. To Casey, despite his disclaimers, this was the World Series. Before more than 6,000 fans, a big crowd for Saint Pete, he won it in the last of the ninth as Joe Christopher tripled and scored on Richie Ashburn's pinch-hit single.

Suddenly, Stengel's mood changed. "Oh, it was just lovely," he chortled. "It's terrific and it should be very good for the players. This will make the Mets believe that if you can beat a great team like the Yankees you should be able to defeat numerous clubs in our league."

Up in New York, the Met victory was greeted as if it really meant something. "Casey's Mets Whip Yanks, 4-3," headlined the New York *Daily News* in type generally reserved for declarations of war and triple ax murders. The sports mob at Toots Shor's restaurant went wild over Casey's revenge. And, at the posh Waldorf-Astoria Hotel, the man who started it all, Bill Shea, was escorting an envoy from one of Africa's new nations down a receiving line to meet Mayor Wagner.

"Boy, wasn't that something about the Mets beating the Yankees?" the ambassador whispered to Shea.

"Yeah," Shea said after giving the ambassador, in his flowing tribal gown, a double take, "but how do you know about that?"

"Well, before our country got its independence, I was the head elevator operator at the Hotel Theresa in Harlem," the ambassador replied.

Five days later the Mets and Yanks met in a rematch at Fort Lauderdale. By a strange coincidence, the Yankees had all their regulars ready to go a full nine innings. They won, 3-2. As the Mets headed north to open their first season after compiling a pretty good record in exhibition games, Stengel warned, "We wouldn't've done so good if their teams was trying."

The Mets' regular season began on the road, in St. Louis. There was another omen the day before their opening, when sixteen players were stuck between floors in a Chase Hotel elevator for twenty minutes. Roger Craig was distraught. "The first time in my life I'm scheduled to open a season, I get stuck in an elevator. We'll probably be stuck here for twenty-four hours," he whined in his North Carolina drawl.

But Hobie Landrith was even more distraught. "It's not so bad for you guys but I'm not built high enough. I can't get any air," the 5-foot-8 receiver complained.

Unfortunately, the Mets were rescued in time to open the season. They lost, 11-4. Craig lasted only three innings and drew the defeat, the first of many. The Mets made three errors, the first of many. And Gil Hodges hit a home run, one of the last of many.

The Mets also lost their second game and then they came home, to the ghostly, decaying Polo Grounds. Don Zimmer was supposed to be their third-baseman and he had a reputation as a gritty, hard-nosed ballplayer who had missed greatness only because of a couple of beanings early in his career. He didn't want to get hit in the head again.

The Mets' beer sponsor had installed a brilliant sign just below the Mets' scoreboard in center field. The first time he took batting practice with the lights on, the 5-foot-9 Zimmer knew he was doomed. The ball came at him right out of the lights. "Fellers, I've had it here," he told his teammates and he proceeded to prove it, setting what still stands as a team record by going hitless thirty-four straight times at bat.* Typical of the Mets, the day after Zimmer got a hit to break out of his slump, he was traded to the Reds for Cliff Cook, another third-baseman, and a left-handed pitcher named Robert G. Miller. The middle initial is important.

Cook had one weakness as a third-baseman. He had a bad back. It only hurt when he bent over to field a ground ball. Miller wasn't

* Tommie Agee tied Zimmer's record in 1968.

much more of an asset on the field, but at least he brought out the best in Lou Niss, the traveling secretary. You see, the Mets already had a pitcher named Miller, Robert L. Miller. How to avoid confusion? Niss had an inspiration. He would put both of them in the same room and may the better man get the best of the phone calls. The incumbent Miller was a right-hander. His middle initial was L., as in "Lefty." Of course he had to be Righty Miller. In the world of the Mets this would make sense.*

Lefty Miller was a typical Met, here today, knocked out of the box tomorrow. Righty Miller was even more typical. A $125,000 draft selection, he lost twelve games in a row for the Mets. On the next-to-the-last day of the season, he finally pitched a complete game and beat the Cubs, 2-1, for his only victory. Charlie Dressen was scouting that game for the Dodgers, and his glowing report persuaded Los Angeles to trade for the erratic right-hander. Miller went on to become a valued big-league relief pitcher, and the Mets ended up with two more frauds.

After nine straight losses had settled them into a seven-year rut, the Mets finally won, beating the Pirates, 9-1. "Break up the Mets," said Joe Ginsberg, a catcher, as he rushed into the clubhouse.

The winning pitcher was Jay Hook, a handsome, bright, and sensitive graduate engineer who had been obtained from the pennant-winning Reds as a $125,000 selection in the expansion draft. Hook could tell you why a curve ball curved, but too often his didn't. Earlier that spring Stengel had let Hook stay in an exhibition game to absorb a brutal beating at the hands of the Orioles. In six innings, he gave up sixteen runs, seventeen hits, four walks, and five home runs. In the sixth inning alone he gave up nine hits and eight runs. After finally being relieved, he cried and tossed things about in the clubhouse. "Why wouldn't you get mad out on the mound when you can do something about it?" Stengel asked.

Hook would win seven more games for the Mets in 1962 . . . and lose nineteen.

Three days after Hook's initial victory, the Mets made a minor trade, obtaining catcher Harry Chiti for "a player to be named later." The following month, Chiti was returned to Cleveland as "the player to be named later." Ron Taylor, later a Met, was with Cleveland at the time. "I always wondered who got the better of that deal," he later quipped.

---

* This year the Mets led the league in Millers. The next season they would lead the league in Dukes—Snider and Carmel.

Players kept coming and going and the Mets kept losing. At one point after their opening debacle, they won eleven of eighteen games for eighth place and a 12-19 record. Then they lost seventeen in a row to establish themselves firmly as the worst collection of peacetime ballplayers ever assembled.

However, in early May, George M. Weiss announced that Met fortunes were changing. For cash, he had been able to steal away from the Orioles one of the finest young hopes in baseball history, a player whom Yankee Manager Ralph Houk had labeled a few years earlier as "the best prospect in the minor leagues." That man was Marv Throneberry, and his credentials weren't the only fraud involved in the so-called cash-only deal. A month later, Hobie Landrith, who by then had caught his breath after the elevator incident, was sent to Baltimore to complete the trade.

> *While the Mets were getting Throneberry, another left-handed-hitting first-baseman at James Monroe High in the Bronx was breaking home run records set thirty years before by Hall-of-Famer Hank Greenberg. Greenberg never hit more than seven home runs in one year for Monroe; Ed Kranepool would hit nine.*

Perhaps Throneberry once had been a great prospect, but time on the bench had eroded whatever skills he had started with. He now was a big, balding, heavy-chested twenty-eight-year-old whose best years were behind him and they weren't much. The real horror was that Throneberry was the best first-baseman the Mets had, pushing such as Ed Bouchee and the sore-kneed Hodges to the bench.

Now that he had a chance to play, Throneberry, as with so many Mets before and after, had his flaws exposed. Fans quickly elected him Mr. Met. It took a while before Throneberry accepted the role and even then he needed help. The transformation took place one night when Throneberry committed an error that allowed the Mets to lose to the Pirates in the fourteenth inning. At this time, Throneberry was still a typical ballplayer, complaining about the official scorer's decision. "How could you call that an error?" he exploded angrily.

"Ah, come on, Marv, you know it was an error," Richie Ashburn joshed from the next locker.

"Yeah, I guess so," Throneberry admitted . . . and he laughed. And so did everybody else. Marvelous Marv Throneberry was born.

Whoops! Marvelous Marv Throneberry fails to come up
with a wide throw and the runner is safe.

The creation of Richie Ashburn, who fed him straight lines,
Throneberry became a symbol of the Mets to the extent that he
doggedly defended his role. "What are you trying to do, steal my
fans?" he asked a teammate who had dropped a critical pop fly.

Throneberry reached his glorious peak during a Decoration Day
doubleheader when he hit into a couple of double plays, struck out
a few times with men on base, and then hit a triple that would
have won the game only to be called out for failing to touch second
base. Stengel rushed out to argue with the umpire over the call,
but was brought up short as he passed his coach, Cookie Lavagetto.
"Forget it, Case," Lavagetto counseled wearily. "He didn't touch
first base, either."

*About the time Throneberry was missing bases, the Mets
signed a young halfback at Alabama A&M where he had
scored seventeen touchdowns in two seasons. Asked what there
was about him that had attracted baseball scouts as well, Cleon
Jones wrote modestly, "outstanding ability."*

Throneberry inspired a devoted following. One day several young fans showed up in T shirts that spelled out M-A-R·V. When they decided to cavort about the dugout, they were ejected from the park. So they paid their way back in to sit in the bleachers. The Mets weren't always so receptive to the banner-carriers, and it took determined efforts by sportswriters to make the Weiss-Grant management embrace what columnist Dick Young of the New York *Daily News* had dubbed the New Breed of fans.

These fans will never forget some of the all-time great Mets who appeared in the Polo Grounds in 1962. One of the greatest was Choo-Choo Coleman, the low-ball catcher whom Stengel tried to create into a legend just as he had done with Yogi Berra. Trouble was, ol' Chooch couldn't hit like Yogi or match his unheralded skill at calling a game. Pitchers just didn't have confidence in Coleman. How could he remember opposition hitters when he forgot the names of his own teammates? He called everybody "Bub." Coleman and Charlie Neal roomed together in 1962. When they met again the next spring, Neal challenged Coleman, "I bet you don't even know who I am."

"Sure I do," Coleman replied. "You're No. 4."

Looking desperately for catching, the Mets in mid-July bought an ex-Dodger from the Giants. In his last time at bat for the Mets at the end of the season, Joe Pignatano hit into a triple play. Even then the Mets continued to lose ground. They ended their own season sixty games out of first place. But this year there was a National League playoff, which dropped the Mets another half game off the pace.

Choo-Choo Coleman, of course, was just one of many misfits with the Mets—and better than most. At least he gave the fans a laugh now and then and some hustle and the thrill of a foul home run.

Still, there were some bona fide big-leaguers in that first group of Mets.

Frank Thomas, abrasive in personality and slow-moving afoot, was one of them. His thirty-four homers are still a club record. He always tried and he'd play outfield, first base, or third and help stewardesses serve meals on charter flights. His "G'n-eat?" was a command, not a request. He also won bets by catching baseballs with his bare hands. Most Met pitchers didn't provide a real test.

Jim Hickman was also in that first group. A sweet guy, mild of manner, he could play all over the diamond, too. This versatility, plus a modicum of power—and expansion—kept him in the majors years longer than he expected. His forte was taking the called third strike, and Stengel once threatened, "If you don't start swinging I'll swing you right out of the lineup." Hilly-Billy, as the Tennessean was called, would fall into bottomless batting slumps, and sometimes his concentration was suspect. In one game, Stengel vainly tried to get Hickman's attention in center field. But Hilly-Billy was busy watching an airplane fly overhead. "I hope you memorized the number on that airplane because that's the one that's taking you to Buffalo," Stengel told him dryly as the inning ended.

Stengel was always threatening to "back up the truck" and send the team en masse to the minors, but he knew the replacements would be worse. ("The best thing that can happen to the Mets is a plane crash. They're the only team that can be strengthened by baseball's disaster plan," one cynical writer observed.)

The pitchers weren't too bad. Little Al Jackson, an awfully nice man, pitched four shutouts. And Roger Craig won ten games, one-fourth of the team's total. He also lost twenty-four, but, he pointed out, "You've got to be a pretty good pitcher to lose twenty or more games. If you're really bad they stop using you." Craig, like Richie Ashburn, who even played some second base before taking his .306 batting average and fleeing to a radio job, also performed above the call of duty for Stengel. He started and he pitched long and short relief. When a bad back kept Craig from making a road trip, Stengel complained, "I left my pitching staff at home."

"The losing isn't so bad, it's the not winning that kills you," Craig would say as he doggedly went out to try again.

The Hearst newspapers were holding their annual Sandlot Classic, pitting top young players from New York against an All-Star team chosen from around the nation. When they held their first workouts in New York for the 1962 game, the catcher for the U.S. All-Stars impressed his teammates by doing push-ups with another player on his back. The muscular sandlotter was Jerry Grote.

Craig's greatest contribution to the Mets would not be realized for some time, however. He and Gil Hodges were roommates on

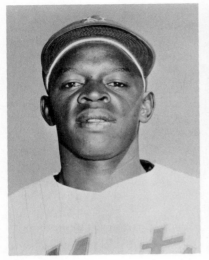

Al Jackson   Richie Ashburn

the road, and Gil knew his playing career was almost over. He
wanted to manage, and the one field in which his knowledge was
limited was pitching. Craig filled that void. Every night, Hodges
would pick his roommate's brains. What about this situation, what
about that? How do pitchers think, live, breathe? When the Mets
made their miracle seven years later, Hodges' handling of his pitching staff would be flawless.

5

Casey

Maybe the Mets were transients and frauds, but through those try
ing times, as sure as dropped fly balls and called third strikes, their
fans could count on Casey Stengel. Day after day, this gnomelike
septuagenarian would trudge out to home plate, one hand holding
a lineup card, the other stuffed deep in his back pocket. His uniform bore a huge "37" on the back. His blue cap was scrunched
down on his head, and it appeared as if only the intrusion of a
huge pair of ears prevented it from sliding down over his eyes.
Those ears were at least two sizes too big for the rest of Casey
Stengel's face, a craggy expanse of wrinkles made up of at least
two parts rubber and one part twinkle to abet the famous wink
captured in a thousand photographs.

It was a face you'd think only a mother, a wife, or a cartoonist
could love, but not so. This face turned on the whole Met generation, from oldsters who could envision themselves still in uniform,
too, to kiddies who unlocked a special warmth in his smile.

It was a face that launched a thousand quips and stopped at
least one nightclub act. (Robert Goulet was appearing in the Chase
Hotel's supper club in St. Louis one night. The Mets were off, so
Casey and his writers took in the show. Goulet came on with a
rousing opener, but his second number was a romantic tune during
which the lights dimmed and he moved along the edge of the stage
to croon directly to the ladies at ringside. Very intimate. Until he
got to Stengel, who turned on "the face" and reduced the veteran
entertainer to sputtering jelly. "Well, people say I'm pretty sexy

myself," Casey announced as the crowd roared with laughter and Goulet struggled to compose himself.)

It was a face that meant the Mets, but there was a lot more to Casey Stengel than just another pretty face.

America had just turned into the twentieth century but it was still a long way from joining the rest of the world. Something like World War I could not even be imagined by the innocents who populated this country's still largely rural Midwest.

Kansas City, Missouri. Wide, tree-lined streets; old frame houses; the horse not yet completely exiled to the race track and show ring. There's a youngster attending Central High named Charles Dillon Stengel. Later they called him "Casey," after his hometown; then he was known as "Dutch." He was captain of the high school football team until a player was killed and the school dropped the sport. He played basketball, too. And baseball. (As Casey liked to say when relating a wild story in which the corroborating participants had passed away, "You could look it up.")

Living catty-corner across the street from the Stengels was the family of one Charles Augustus Nichols. They called him "Kid Nichols" then, and in the baseball archives, and he was a big-league pitcher who won 360 games. At that time, only two men had won more, the legendary Cy Young and Pud Galvin, and all three are in baseball's Hall of Fame. You could look that up, too. Kid Nichols briefly owned a minor-league franchise in Kansas City, but he was usually sitting on his porch when the teen-age Dutch Stengel got home from school, and they'd talk baseball.

By 1910, Dutch Stengel was nineteen years old, had finished high school, and was going off to play pro baseball for Kankakee, Illinois. He asked Kid Nichols, who was then forty-one, for some wisdom to pack in his grip.

"Take all the advice anybody gives you," said Nichols, who had managed the Cardinals for a year and a half. "Hold it in your head for thirty days and try it out. Then, if it doesn't fit your shoes, let it out the other ear. But never tell anybody that their advice didn't help you."

(Half a century later, Casey would be reminded of Kid Nichols. Warren Spahn was winding up his career with the Mets and had just posted his 361st pitching victory to pass Nichols on the all-time winning list. "Did you ever know Kid Nichols?" a young reporter asked Stengel. "A big right-hander who threw over the top," said Casey without a minute's hesitation. "He's dead at the present time, and he lived across the street from me in Kansas City. Why did you want to know?")

Stengel was to make a lot of money out of baseball, and he invested it wisely through the years. But his first excursion into pro ball was a financial disaster. The Northern Association, of which Kankakee was a leading member, folded at midseason, and Stengel had to depart without his final paycheck. They let him keep his uniform, though, and, he recalled, "It wasn't much of a uniform, but then, it wasn't much of a check, either."

Stengel didn't have to go home for the rest of the summer, however. He transferred his allegiance to Maysville, Kentucky, of the more stable Blue Grass League, where he hit an inconspicuous .223 in sixty-nine games.

The next season, Stengel, a left-handed-hitting outfielder, batted a more promising .352 for Aurora, Illinois, in the Wisconsin-Illinois circuit, and 1912 brought a promotion to Montgomery, Alabama, of the old Southern League. Near the end of that season his batting average was .290, and he was purchased by the Brooklyn Dodgers. Before he was through, he would wear the uniform of every New York team.

That call to the majors ended any dreams by Mrs. Stengel that her boy would become a dentist. Casey did indeed attend dental college for a while after high school, and there are two leading theories on why he quit. One was the absence of any left-handed dental equipment, the other that, as a dentist, he could talk to only one person at a time.

Casey broke in with the Dodgers with four straight base hits at the tag end of the 1912 season, and that earned him total ostracism from his new teammates. In keeping with the custom of the time, to protect their own jobs, the veterans would freeze rookies out of batting practice. After a couple of days, the irrepressible Stengel had business cards printed on which he introduced himself as a bona fide member of the team and requested the right to practice his hitting.

Casey and the big leagues were made for each other, and he embraced the swashbuckling, freewheeling life with relish. Once he silenced a group of bleacher hecklers by hiding a pigeon under his cap and then tipping it to "give them the bird" as he trotted out to take his fielding position. He had his own style of hazing new players, too. Back in Stengel's playing days, the hayseed rookie had not yet become an anachronism. Casey loved to offer to take a new man back to his hotel on the New York subway, then, as now, a terrifying experience for any stranger. Then, when they got to a busy station, Stengel would nimbly hop off as the doors were closing, leaving his panic-stricken companion to find his own way home. The kid would be lucky to make it by the next day's game.

Casey spent five full seasons with the old Dodgers, helping them to a National League championship in 1916. Before he was traded to Pittsburgh for the 1918 season, Casey's career suffered a minor interruption for navy duty. This was one time that Casey, who loved to describe himself as "slick," outsmarted himself. For some infraction at the end of the season, Stengel was due to get a $50 fine from the National League office. Confident that they'd never fine a serviceman, and convinced by a recruiting officer that the war would be over in thirty days, Casey, then twenty-eight, joined the navy. Imagine his chagrin when he realized he was saving the fine but had blown several months' salary. At least that's Casey's story.

Stengel did manage to get some of the money back, however. During his hitch at the Brooklyn Navy Yard, he organized a team of shore-based sailors, and they'd challenge the crew of each ship to a game when it came into port. There was a lot of betting on the games, so Casey made sure to schedule them as soon after the ship docked as possible. That way opposition players wouldn't have a chance to get their land legs back. Yes, Casey was slick.

After being released from the service, Stengel played for the Pirates, the Phillies, the Giants, and the Braves. He helped the Giants win a pennant both seasons he played for them and batted well over .300 each year. But that wasn't the best thing he accomplished in the Polo Grounds.

For it was at that ball park, to which he returned with the Mets forty years later, that Stengel met Miss Edna Lawson, a striking young woman who was to become his wife. Edna at the time was engaged to a boy in California, but she was visiting friends and relatives in New York and her girl friend was going with one of the Giants. "Casey won't tell you this," she confided once with a warm smile, "but the Giants [John J. McGraw was the manager] used to take Casey out for defense in the late innings. So he always dressed

early, and we got to know each other while we were waiting for
the game to end."

A year later, while Casey was playing for the Braves, he and his
Edna were married. Stengel was thirty-three then, and his in-laws
were a little upset about the match. They hadn't met Casey, but
they had read in the sports pages that he was considered an "old
outfielder." Edna had to explain that this meant baseball old, not
old old.

Stengel tried to play the next year for the Braves, but he managed only one hit in thirteen tries, and his major-league career came
to an end. Over fourteen seasons, he showed a .284 lifetime average,
plus a .393 batting record in three World Series. However, while
his batting eye may have dimmed and speed diminished, the
Braves knew Casey was still slick. They named him playing manager of their Eastern League farm team at Worcester, Massachusetts, and he and Edna spent their first anniversary riding the team
bus to a road game.

From Worcester, Casey went to Toledo, where he played a little,
owned a piece of the club, and managed the Mud Hens to one
pennant in six years. His big achievement there was in keeping the
club afloat, especially after the stock market crash, by rehabilitating
older ball players and selling them back to the majors at a tremendous profit.

In 1934, Casey himself went to the majors as manager of the
helpless Dodgers, who finished sixth, fifth, and then seventh during
his tenure. Even as a manager, he retained his biting sense of
humor. One day the Dodgers were opening a series in Philadelphia's tiny Baker Bowl, and writers covering the club, instead of
going down early with the team, waited until the last minute and
took a train directly to the ball park. Stengel, frustrated at not
having his usual traveling audience, was further annoyed when the
writers showed up just before game time and immediately began
criticizing his choice of Walter (Boom-Boom) Beck as starting
pitcher. He was further chagrined when Beck made the writers look
good by showing everybody why they called him Boom-Boom. As
Casey went out to relieve his pitcher, Beck disagreed with the
decision. In anger, he heaved the ball against the Baker Bowl's
tin fence. Out in right field, Hack Wilson was using the brief
respite to take a little nap, his hands on his knees, after a late night
on the town. As the ball hit the fence with a bang, old Hack awoke

with a start, fielded the carom, and fired a perfect throw in to second.

The writers were howling in the press box, but Casey had the last laugh. "It was the day of the trading deadline, so I told 'em we had a big deal cooking and made 'em sit up with me all night. I made 'em buy the booze, too," he related with a leer and a wink.

The Dodgers fired Stengel after the 1936 season but still had to pay him for 1937, as provided in his contract. In 1938 he went up to manage the Braves, another collection of Sad Sacks. (The maitre d' at the Chase Hotel supper club was one of his old Boston batting-practice pitchers, incidentally.) Casey's best finish there in six years was a fifth and, when he was hit by a cab and broke his leg one summer, an acidulous sportswriter nominated the driver as "the man who has done the most for sports in Boston this year." Casey forgave the cabby, but not the writer.

After being let out in Boston following the 1943 season, Casey went back to the minors. He won a pennant at Milwaukee, finished seventh at Kansas City, and then moved out to Oakland, where he owned a piece of the club, and finished second, fourth, and first.

It was at this point, after the 1948 season, that George Weiss called on him to manage the Yankees. Casey's managing record in the majors had been a little less than mediocre, but Weiss realized it had been the fault of the teams' personnel. He saw through Casey's clowning and realized this man could be one of the great managers.

Casey liked it in California, but Weiss persuaded him to come East. With the Yankees, Stengel would be able to earn vindication for those frustrating years in Boston and Brooklyn, and, as it turned out, he vindicated himself right into the Hall of Fame.*

It was this same pride and desire for vindication that spurred Casey to accept the second call from Weiss to manage the Mets after the Yankees had thrown him out. Why would a man of seventy-one return to the rigors of coast-to-coast all-hours travel with a team he knew would be terrible? ("If anybody asks for me, I'm being embalmed," Stengel once muttered as he shuffled off to his Houston hotel room after a dawn arrival from a night game in

---

* Rules of the Hall of Fame stipulate a five-year waiting period after a man's baseball career has ended. This was waived in Stengel's case, and he was inducted into the baseball shrine in 1966, the year after he quit managing at seventy-five. "It's better than on a grave. I'm getting in there now when I can know what it really means," he said with feeling.

California.) Most people Casey's age would be happy to enjoy a comfortable retirement. "Most people my age are dead," Stengel replied, and that was that.

With the Yankees, Stengel had become famous for his "platooning," and it was Bill Veeck who credited him with thus inventing the concept of a twenty-five-man team. (A concept, incidentally, used just as successfully by Gil Hodges during the pennant-winning season of 1969.)

While platooning the Yankees to their ten pennants, Stengel acknowledged that not all the players liked his regime. Gene Woodling, a left-handed batter, particularly hated being platooned against certain pitchers. He left the Yankees nursing a loud and bitter hatred of the old man. But later he realized that being platooned had enabled him to enjoy a much longer and more successful (and profitable) career than he ever could have hoped for otherwise. Woodling even served a brief term with the Mets, and, later, as a coach with the Orioles, he would direct any mutual friends who showed up in Baltimore to "give Case my best when you see him. I owe him plenty."

With the Mets, Stengel was forced to continue his platooning, not so much to make the most of strength but to cover up weakness. The expansion draft had provided the Mets with virtually no complete ball players. If they all hadn't had a critical flaw of some kind, they'd still have been with their original clubs. And Casey got to the point where he was fed up with new ball players complaining they could have been regulars where they came from, only the manager was in love with the man who played ahead of them at the position. "People who complain about bad luck have bad luck all their lives," he snorted.

During his years of managing, Casey also developed a unique brand of double-talk that was soon dubbed "Stengelese." The trademarks of Stengelese were the complete absence of proper names—it was always "that feller" or "the outfielder"—and the use of a verbal shorthand in which whole paragraphs were telescoped with two or three sentences completely eliminated. (Thus, when Casey commented on the Mets winning the pennant, "They did it slow, but fast," a student of Stengelese knew immediately that he meant it had taken the Mets a long time to get going, but they certainly arrived with a rush.)

Stengelese was a game he'd play with the traveling crew he

Casey Stengel, a hero to fans of all ages.

anointed as "my writers." Nosy strangers would get an even worse version, but he would talk straight to those in the middle category who might want honestly to know what he thought of his team in spring training and who was going to play where. Sometimes his own writers would try to eavesdrop on those sessions.

Once you learned all Casey's terms of reference, Stengelese was almost intelligible. Never completely intelligible, though, because Casey had a reason for this near-gibberish. Any conclusions drawn from his monologues had to be drawn by the writer, thus Casey could avoid complete blame for statements that might backfire.

Stengel liked to pretend a weakness on names. ("The old man

may not know names, but he sure knows how they should be pitched to and where they should be played," one-time Met outfielder Richie Ashburn marveled.) And while he didn't call all his writers by name, he knew the paper each worked for, whether it was an afternoon or morning daily, when its deadlines fell, and what sort of story appealed to different reporters.

Stengel was intensely loyal to his regular crew, which helped explain his near-unanimous editorial approval. Radio-TV and magazine types who came barging in seeking extra time would be asked, "Where was you when we play a doubleheader in Houston?"

Like most managers, Stengel was an egotist. The center of the stage was the only place to be. Nobody ever succeeded in shouldering him out of the spotlight.

His stamina was amazing, not even considering his age and the backbreaking road trips. He'd drink his writers under and then be up at dawn for a huge breakfast while the younger men were still sleeping off massive hangovers. Only after he quit managing did he develop an ulcer. "It's about forty years overdue," an old friend noted. Typically, though, any reporters who lasted the night would be rewarded with a news tip. Some of them were real goodies.

Stengel was never close to his players on a personal basis, although he and Edna, probably because they were childless themselves, had a warm feeling for the younger ones. (Mrs. Stengel, especially, tried to help the frightened young brides of the rookies as they struggled through the discomforts and uncertainties of their first spring training.)

Casey, for his part, announced to players on the first day of camp: "I do my drinking in the hotel bar, so if you're gonna drink, pick someplace else. It would be a shame if I caught you and had to send you down to Buffalo." Generally, Casey ran a loose ship. He figured dissipation took its own toll.

Casey could be raw and abrasive. Sensitive players like the Yankees' Norm Siebern cracked under his sarcasm. But Stengel never yelled at a player he didn't feel was capable of doing better, and although occasionally abrupt and rude, he showed great flashes of consideration, especially to old players of his generation. He would save his comic and newsworthy routines for bad losses, to take critical pressure off his players. There were few monologues after a winning game, when there might be a real-live hero to be lionized.

Casey Stengel in a contemplative mood.

And when Richie Ashburn, one of his few bona fide big-leaguers that first season, had a chance to hit .300, Stengel carefully calculated how to keep the veteran from dipping below that figure during the final days of the campaign. After hitting his .306, Ashburn retired, knowing the last entry in his baseball record would be a good one.

For a couple of years, the Mets had a pitcher named Galen Cisco, who had been captain of Ohio State's 1958 Rose Bowl team. At Ohio State, Cisco had played for Woody Hayes, a giant in the football coaching profession.

Hayes and Stengel were a lot alike, Cisco said once. An ability for total recall of past games and situations was one thing they had in common. Although the players changed in college, Hayes was always able to remember how certain coaches reacted in different situations. Stengel remembered ball players the same way, and that was the secret behind some of his apparently bizarre substitutions.

(Once, though, with the Mets, he put together a weird lineup against the Cubs in Chicago, apparently flouting all his old lefty-righty tenets. The patchwork group proceeded to whale the Cubs, 19-1, and only later did Stengel point out that the Mets had been involved in a lot of recent doubleheaders and the team he was playing was his "rested platoon." Incidentally, that game produced one of the all-time gems of Metsiana. A fan, obviously playing in the office run pool, called a newspaper in Connecticut that evening. "How many runs did the Mets score today?" he asked. Told they had scored nineteen runs, he then blurted, "Great! Did they win?")

Cisco, however, added one even more important characteristic Hayes and Stengel shared. "Both of them go into every game convinced they can win. And no matter how far behind they fall, they keep trying to win until the very end of the game. No matter how bad our team is going, Casey comes out to the ball park every day looking for some way he can help himself win the game."

Maybe a lot of Mets were going through the motions in those early days, but nobody could say that about the manager. He was definitely a lot more than just another pretty face.

6

Hunt for a Second-Baseman

The Mets decided to put second things first as they entered the 1963 season. They needed a second-baseman and, when training camp opened, there were no less than seven potential candidates for the job.

Among the holdovers were Hot Rod Kanehl, Elio Chacon, and Charlie Neal, but the latter two were really considered stronger possibilities at shortstop. The four new Keystone (as in Kops) hopefuls were Elijah Jeremiah (Pumpsie) Green, Larry Burright, Ted Schreiber, and Ron Hunt.

Green's major claim to fame was that when Gene Conley, a 6-foot 9-inch pitcher, jumped the Red Sox one year, ostensibly to visit Israel, Green disappeared into a Boston traffic jam with him. The Mets got Pumpsie, along with shortstop Al Moran and pitcher Tracy Stallard, in a winter deal for Felix Mantilla, a reluctant warrior who had once told the Braves, "Rest me or trade me."

Burright also had been obtained in a deal in company with first-baseman Tim Harkness from the Dodgers in exchange for Bob (Righty) Miller. Burright had been a starter for the contending Dodgers in the first half of 1962, and the Mets soon learned why he had been benched. Although he couldn't hit, he also had a habit for making late-inning errors afield. Harkness, a Canadian who was a former hockey player, was billed as a defensive specialist because he played first base in late innings for the Dodgers. He was a good glove man only in comparison with the man he replaced, elephantine Frank Howard. "That Bavasi," Casey Stengel said in anger,

54

Ron Hunt in typical action, diving for a wide throw as
Roy Sievers of the Phillies steals second.

and admiration, when he realized the Dodger general manager had
trimmed him again. "He plays this Harshman [sic] in the last
innings for two years so I'll think he can field and will buy him."

Schreiber was bought by the Mets in the first round of the
December draft from the Red Sox organization for $25,000.* Hunt
was another of George Weiss's conditional installment purchases
from the Braves. He cost the Mets $5,000 down and they would
have to come up with another $35,000 if he stuck through the first
month of the season. Knowing how the Mets nursed Mrs. Payson's
dollars, it was no surprise that they tried out all their other candidates before giving Hunt a shot. He turned out to represent the
best $40,000 they ever spent, not necessarily excluding a similar
sum they later surrendered for Tom Seaver.

* The Mets often made more than one error on the same ball. Schreiber was
an example of how one man, Johnny Murphy, could make two errors on one
ballplayer. He had recommended Schreiber's original signing with the Red Sox
and it was he who suggested the Mets draft him. When Murphy got better at
picking players, so did the Mets.

Hunt, from St. Louis, originally was signed by the Braves as a third-baseman for a $20,000 bonus. However, when their second-baseman, Red Schoendienst, was stricken with tuberculosis in 1959, the Braves shifted all their best minor-league prospects to that spot as protection. Hunt had three fairly ordinary minor-league seasons until he got to Austin, where he made the 1962 Texas League All-Star Team, batted .309, and impressed Met coach Solly Hemus, who had been detached from the parent team on a scouting mission. The turning point in Hunt's career came when a minor-league manager, Jimmy Brown, taught him to throw sidearm to first base when turning over a double play. "If you throw it low, the base runner's got to start sliding early, otherwise you'll hit him right between the eyes. That's the only way to protect yourself," Brown told his aggressive pupil.

Hunt played the game hard, tough, and recklessly—when he played. He suffered from all sorts of allergies and was prone to injury. The Mets finally came up with an allergist who gave Hunt the right injections so he didn't have to sneeze his way through a baseball season, but they couldn't keep him from getting hurt. He was sick for the 1963 opener and hurt his finger playing handball the next winter and was out for the beginning of 1964, too. Then he suffered a shoulder separation. The highlight of his medical career came after he had been traded to the Dodgers. While getting treatment for one injury, which was almost healed, he fell off the rubbing table and hurt himself again.

But when he was in the lineup, Hunt injected a new excitement into the often lethargic Mets. A typical play one night in Milwaukee: Hunt was thrown out at the plate trying to score from second on a double-play grounder. Hunt, out by 10 feet, went slamming into catcher Ed Bailey in a vain attempt to dislodge the ball, and Bailey came up swinging. Both benches emptied and there was a dandy brawl. One smallish figure in a warmup jacket was noted on the periphery of the crowd, trying to restrain Denis Menke from behind. But the husky shortstop simply shrugged his shoulders and the little figure went flying on his back. That's when people could see who it was. "My God," thought Menke as he recognized the prone septuagenarian, "I've killed Casey Stengel."

Hunt cultivated his aggressive reputation, but he loved the Met fans and it was reciprocated. He was a favorite of Mrs. Payson's, too, and one winter she personally vetoed a deal that would have

Duke Snider (left) and Tracy Stallard had their differences.

sent Hunt to the Minnesota Twins. The memory pictures remain of Hunt as a Met: No. 33 sprawling in the dirt diving for a base hit just out of reach; Ron taking a pitch on the back to get on base and start a rally; or the little second-baseman glaring out from under his cap as he signed dozens of autographs before a game.

There were a couple of other new faces around, too, including one topped with a familiar crown of completely gray hair: Duke Snider, long-time hero of the Dodgers, had been purchased by the Mets late in spring training. Now thirty-six, he gave the Mets some exciting moments early in the season, including his four hundredth career home run.

But the Duke of Flatbush was never happy with the Mets. After all his great years with championship Dodger teams, he felt his tour with the Mets was demeaning. Almost from the day he arrived, he tried to stir up another trade that would take him to a pennant contender. He didn't hit a home run after July 14, and the next spring he did get his wish by being sold to the Giants. On his departure he blasted the Mets as "a bunch of clowns."

Tracy Stallard, the pitcher, volunteered to answer the charges. "We expected a lot from Duke Snider. We all looked up to him and we expected him to be a leader, but he wasn't. If we were such a lousy ball club, he should remember that he was one-twenty-fifth of that ball club," Stallard said during an informal "press conference" on the team bus to the ball park one afternoon.

Although he and Snider later made up, Stallard never backed down on his charges. Given an opportunity to claim he was misquoted, the handsome Virginian drawled evenly, "If you read it in the paper, I said it." A class declaration.

Roger Craig was the Mets' opening-day pitcher in 1963 for the second year in a row, and this time the inaugural was held at home in the Polo Grounds away from the balky hotel elevators of St. Louis. Burright was at second for the ailing Hunt and Duke Snider played center field. Craig, Charlie Neal, and Frank Thomas were the only repeaters from the lineup that had opened in 1962.

The big surprise was the right-fielder, a big eighteen-year-old rookie who had been given $85,000 to sign the previous summer as a first-baseman, Ed Kranepool. Kranepool had played a little outfield in high school and he had a fine throwing arm. Stengel always liked to take a chance by finessing a youngster into the lineup. Maybe Kranepool could make it right away?

The Mets had signed the left-handed-hitting youngster out of James Monroe High in the Bronx in competition with almost every other major-league club. One stipulation of his agreement with the new team was that he be taken on a West Coast road trip. The Mets agreed, but balked at sending publicity man Tom Meany along as a baby-sitter. So Kranepool spent most of the trip sitting in hotel lobbies.

Kranepool's father had been killed in World War II and he was brought up by his mother. Only his body was mature when he joined the Mets, but partly for gate appeal and partly because the veterans weren't much better, he was rushed into the majors before he was ready. The pressure forced him into an undemonstrative—almost sullen—shell, and when Duke Snider offered him some batting tips, he snapped, "You know, you're not having such a good year yourself." That finished Kranepool with the veterans.

The $85,000 price tag made people expect a superstar, and they turned on Eddie to vent their own disappointment when it developed that all he would become was a better-than-fair major-leaguer who could hit with some power and field his position.

"What do they want? Why don't they get off my back?" Kranepool would complain as one of the famous New Breed banners asked, "Is Ed Kranepool Over the Hill?" He was nineteen years old at the time. The problem with Eddie was that he had a slow body as well as a slow bat. Even when he was hustling, it looked as if

Ed Kranepool

he were running in quicksand. And when he didn't try, which
happened, he couldn't disguise it.

Still, when the Mets did become successful, Ed Kranepool was a
part of it. He had paid a price—"If I could have seen ahead in
1962, I would have signed with another club. There was a lot of
frustration through the years." But he also had the satisfaction of
survival. And this one-time outcast has been, for several years, the
team's player-rep.

For all their new faces, the Mets proved just as dismal as in their
inaugural season. As usual, they lost their opening game, 7-0, as
Ernie Broglio of the Cardinals pitched a two-hitter. Both Met hits
were made by Larry Burright, which was not an omen of things to
come. Although these Mets were billed as defensively superior to
their predecessors, they made two errors. This *was* an omen.

There was one bit of improvement, however. The 1962 Mets had
lost their first nine games. The 1963 losing streak was ended at
eight.

There were some bright moments, though. Ron Hunt had an outstanding year and was runner-up in voting for top rookie. Al Jackson won thirteen games. And Jim Hickman hit seventeen home runs.
Duke Snider hit fourteen and played in the All-Star Game.

> *Down in Augusta, Georgia, the Tigers' farm team had just
> won the Sally League's first-half championship under the direc-
> tion of a portly former big-league catcher named Rube Walker.*

There were some magical Met moments, too. Chico Fernandez

was traded to the Mets, joined them on the road, and then had to spend his first night with the team sitting up in the hotel lobby. His new roomie, Choo-Choo Coleman, wouldn't let him in. Charlie Neal, who seemed to have lost his competitive zeal when he left the Dodgers, was traded off and, on May 22, Gil Hodges was sent to Washington as manager. In return, the Mets received Jim Piersall, an eccentric—to say the least—outfielder. Piersall's greatest moment with the Mets was his last. He hit his hundredth career home run in the Polo Grounds and to celebrate ran around the bases backward. Stengel was mortified by what he considered an unprofessional stunt, and grew even more angry when he learned that Piersall had disabled himself by pulling a leg muscle during his backward jaunt. Piersall soon found himself "fired" by baseball's worst team.*

The trouble with the Mets in 1963 was that they never "commenced"† getting good, and poor Roger Craig lost eighteen games in a row en route to his 5-and-22 record. He even tried switching jerseys with Tracy Stallard to change his luck one game, but it didn't work. When Craig finally won a game to break his streak it was on a home run by Jim Hickman that should have been caught. "While I was losing, I was a celebrity. I don't guess you guys will be coming by any more," Craig said dolefully to the assembled writers. No man, however, had ever borne such a burden with more dignity. Craig was a loser only as a pitcher, not as a man.

Down in Johnstown, Pennsylvania, the annual American Amateur Baseball Congress Tournament was under way. His Leone's Restaurant team of Baltimore lost in the finals, but, batting .379 and tying a record with four home runs, Ron Swoboda was the star of the tournament.

The tenth-place Mets did show some final improvement, though. They only lost 111 games compared to 120 the year before, and they had advanced from 60½ games out of first place to 48.

Of more significance, they had drawn over a million fans at home after just missing that figure in their inaugural campaign. The next season they would move into their new stadium in Flushing

---

* In Stengelese, only frauds are "fired." Good players and managers, like himself, are "discharged."

† Things never begin or start in Stengelese, they always "commence."

Meadow and attendance would soar anew even though there was little hope the Mets would do likewise in the standings.

The phenomenon of Met attendance was awe-inspiring. What business did a bad ball club, hopelessly last and playing in a dingy, antiquated stadium with no parking facilities, have drawing over a million people? And a million enthusiastic people? How many masochists could there be in New York?

One answer, of course, was nostalgia. Most New Yorkers had been National League fans, and they were eager to see again their old favorites like Stan Musial, Willie Mays, and Sandy Koufax. The Mets traded shamelessly on this sentiment, and a major portion of their crowds came out to see games against the Giants and the Dodgers.

Still, this didn't account for the enthusiasm with which the team was supported. The real answer was that blasé New Yorkers had taken the Mets to heart as their hometown team, for better or for worse. The cold and efficient Yankees inspired no such love affair. New York, as far as the Mets were concerned, was just a big Green Bay, Wisconsin.

Casey Stengel helped feed this feeling. He was the Mets' best salesman—all over the nation. Crowds trailed him wherever he went, young and old alike. The Mets became "camp," and the Polo Grounds, and later Shea Stadium, became a place to go to have some fun.

One couple during a Sunday doubleheader in 1963 overdid it. Sitting deep in a near-empty section, they took advantage of the distraction of an argument on the field to indulge in their mutual affection. When discovered, they were ejected by stadium police. "But we're married," they protested.

"Why don't you save that stuff for at home?" the special cop asked.

"We can't get any privacy at home because of the kids," the lady replied.

Late in the second game several hours later, the announcer for the visitors' radio station gave out the attendance. "The total crowd for today's doubleheader is 18,844 . . . and only a couple have left," he said.

The famous banners also began to emerge in the Polo Grounds, and eventually they were acknowledged by the management with a special day. The most apropos said, simply, "Pray."

Two of the Mets' more famous fans would sparkle at Shea. One was dubbed the Mad Doctor. A radiologist, Dr. Dominick Principato, would cavort in the mezzanine seats behind home plate wearing a bright-yellow slicker. His cohorts wore yellow hats. They not only preceded Chicago's Bleacher Bums, they sat in more expensive seats. The Mad Doctor even showed up on an occasional road trip.

Another fan celebrity was Karl Ehrhardt, the Sign Man. A commercial artist, Ehrhardt made up hundreds of signs covering all moods and situations, mostly bad, and would bring a selected armload to Shea for various games. But none of his signs could sum up the 1963 season better than Stengel's own succinct comment after the opening-day loss to St. Louis: "We're still a fraud. The attendance got robbed."

7

Into Shea

The Mets found a new place to lose in 1964—Mexico.

At the invitation of the government, the Mets opened their spring training exhibition schedule with a three-game series against Mexican League teams in Mexico City. Naturally, they lost their opener, 6-4, before winning the next two. "Did the high altitude here bother your players?" Casey Stengel was asked after the opening defeat.

"The altitude always bothers my players, even in the Polo Grounds, which is below sea level," the manager replied.

The visit was a tour de force for Stengel. He captivated the Mexicans, who greeted the Mets' arrival with an old City College of New York cheer: "Allagaroo, Allagaroo!" In fact, they almost didn't want to let him leave, but for another reason. Mrs. Stengel had misplaced her tourist permit, and the Mets' charter flight back to Florida was delayed two hours until somebody important could be found to vouch for her.

Partly to get players ready for the early Mexican tour and partly to get a look at some young prospects and improve a few old-timers, the Mets held a special early camp. Casey called it, "My instructural school." Jim Hickman was given a brief course in leadership by being named captain of one of the intrasquad teams and an even briefer course in playing third base, which he flunked just as quickly. Larry Bearnarth went down to learn how to see. The Mets hoped the likable relief pitcher would field his position better if he tried glasses. Some of the youngsters would be heard of later—

Bud Harrelson, who impressed Stengel with his grasp of baseball tactics; Ron Swoboda, who impressed everyone with his raw power; and Dick Selma, a young pitcher with a live arm who was on his honeymoon. Some of them would never be heard of again, like Jerry Hinsley, a baby-faced right-hander the Mets had stolen from the Pirates in the draft who never looked as good again as he did in that early camp.

Some new players the Mets had added over the winter also were invited, including George Altman and Bill Wakefield, who had been obtained in a November trade with St. Louis for Roger Craig. Altman, an outfielder, was handicapped all year with injuries and produced nothing. Wakefield, a relief pitcher, gave the Mets one good year.

Right after the '63 season, the National League had taken pity on the Mets and the Colt .45s and permitted them to draft some extra players for $30,000 each. The Mets took two, first-baseman Bill Haas from the Los Angeles organization and pitcher Jack Fisher from San Francisco. Haas had been a good minor-league hitter but, he confessed, as a fielder and base runner, "I make mental mistakes." Those mistakes proved too glaring even for the Mets. Fisher was a proven major-league pitcher with a tendency to portliness. Even his friends called him Fat Jack.

"When I'm winning, they say I'm husky; when I lose they call me fat," Fat Jack once complained. But he was a hard-nosed professional and he would do a job for you. The Mets had two trainers, and for almost the entire season Fisher was able to fudge on the weekly weight checks required by Stengel by always claiming "the other one weighed me." He'd then report his weight as an optimistic 217 pounds. Late in the year, Fisher went into a long slump. Couldn't win a game. At the last scheduled weigh-in, one of his teammates decided to play a little joke on Fisher. He made him actually get on a scale in front of official witnesses. The needle shot up to 237. The next year the Mets tried to cut Fisher's salary because they felt he had allowed himself to get out of shape late in the season and that was the cause of his slump. They didn't know he had been 237 all year.

Also in the regular camp was a slender and shy young outfielder trying to make the Mets as a conditional purchase from the Braves. Adrian (Pat) Garrett didn't cut it, but, five years

Carl Willey

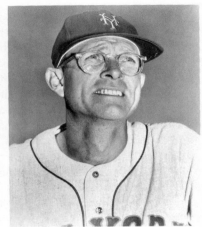

Roy McMillan

Jim Hickman

Jack Fisher

later the Mets tried his kid brother, Wayne, an infielder, whom they drafted from the same organization.

There were some other recruits joining up at various points during the season, like Hawk Taylor, Charley Smith, and Roy McMillan. Taylor had once been given a $125,000 bonus by the Braves. He could run, hit, field, throw, and serve as a catcher, third-baseman, or outfielder. He could do everything, in fact, but play. The total was less than the parts. Hawk had cousins with nicknames like Flop and Duck. Smith was obtained from the White Sox and went hitless his first twenty-six times at bat for the Mets. A third-baseman, he had trouble with slow-hit ground balls, but he hit twenty home runs and struck out over one hundred times. Things were always happening to him or to those close to him that would force Smith to leave the team on urgent business. Sometimes he was slow getting back. He was also afraid of frogs.

McMillan, however, was an outstanding addition. The skinny, quiet Texan from Sam Rayburn's home town of Bonham had long been one of the premier shortstops in the National League and, at thirty-four, he still retained many of his old skills. More important, he was a class person who improved the character of any team.

McMillan always prided himself as a teacher. He boasted how he had helped tutor the young shortstops who had eventually taken over his job at both Cincinnati (Leo Cardenas) and Milwaukee (Denis Menke). When he heard the Mets had a kid prospect named Harrelson, his eyes lit up behind his round-lensed glasses. The next spring he took the youngster in charge. The day Harrelson arrived from his army tour, McMillan called a newspaperman aside. "Does this Harrelson boy have a nickname?" he asked. "It will help if I can call him by name right away." When McMillan's career was ended by a shoulder injury in 1966, he had done his work well. Harrelson was ready. It was no surprise that the Mets retained Roy in their organization, and he quickly became an outstanding minor-league manager.

With the acquisition of Fisher, the Mets approached the season with what they thought would be a pretty good pitching staff. Their four starting pitchers would be Al Jackson, Fisher, Stallard, and Carl Willey.

Willey was expected to be their best pitcher. This gentle man from Maine had been lost in the Milwaukee organization for his entire career before the Mets rescued him in 1963. Although he showed he had not done a lot of pitching for some time, he put together a commendable 9-14 record that included four shutouts. This year the Mets expected better things from the thirty-two-year-old right-hander, and Willey was encouraging those hopes with an outstanding spring in which he did not surrender a single earned run.

On April 3, Willey was pitching in one of his final tuneups against the Tigers in Saint Petersburg. He had gone into the seventh inning, and if he retired Gates Brown for the final out, he would be through for the day. Hawk Taylor, the catcher, called for a changeup, and he sensed trouble as he saw the pitch float in high and out over the plate. It was the kind of pitch a batter hits straight up the middle and Brown did, a vicious line drive that grazed the fingertips of Willey's glove and crashed into his jaw with such force that the ball ricocheted all the way to first base, where Tim Harkness made the putout.

Willey never lost consciousness, but his jaw was broken. All his fine spring work, all the hopes he shared with the Mets, were wiped away. In his attempts to come back too quickly near the end of the year, he hurt his arm. He was never a winning pitcher again.

Their spirits down, the Mets opened the season on the road and, predictably, they lost. But this time their initial losing streak was ended at four. When they got home, they were cheered by the huge new stadium that awaited them. After long delays, many caused by the Mets as they insisted on change after change in the specifications, the dual-purpose stadium with its movable seats was ready. "It's got escalators and ramps and fifty-four bathrooms and we'll steal people away from the World's Fair," Stengel trumpeted, referring to the fact that the opening of Shea coincided with the New York World's Fair situated right across the street.

A total of 48,736 fans showed up for the historic first game on April 17, 1964. Met players complained that the batting background wasn't any good, and they lost to Pittsburgh, 4-3. Stengel pointed out that the Pirates had collected sixteen hits.

Six weeks later, not long after the Mets had scored their epochal 19-1 victory over Chicago, Shea Stadium was really christened with the world's longest doubleheader. Play began at 1:08 P.M. on this Memorial Day Sunday, and the Mets succumbed to the Giants without incident in the first game, 5-3. Then they went out for the second game and they almost never stopped. The contest lasted twenty-three innings and seven hours and twenty-three minutes of playing time. The last out of this thirty-two-inning doubleheader was recorded at 11:25 P.M. as the Mets proved they could also lose in extra innings, 8-6.

The Mets pulled off a triple play in this game; Willie Mays, the peerless center-fielder, had to fill in at shortstop for three innings;

Pee Wee Reese, the former Dodger, had broadcast the first game of a doubleheader in St. Louis and flew to New York in time to see the last couple of innings at Shea; and Ralph Kiner, the Met broadcaster who had left the press box in the eighth to go downstairs for his post-game show, spent fifteen innings in solitude because he never knew when the last out would come.

The weariest Mets of all were catcher Chris Cannizzaro and first-baseman Ed Kranepool. Cannizzaro caught the entire second game and, by one count, had to squat down over three hundred times (for each pitch). Kranepool had reported direct to Shea after being recalled from Buffalo, where he had played in a late doubleheader the night before. The next day he was so tired, he didn't even remember that he had been in the game.

June 21 was Fathers' Day, and just over 32,000 fathers, and fans with fathers, showed up for a doubleheader against the Phillies. Jim Bunning, a noted right-handed father of seven, who since has added more, pitched the first game for the Phillies. He was opposed by Tracy Stallard, which some noted as an omen of big things to come by the opposition. After all, it was Stallard who had surrendered the record sixty-first home run to Roger Maris in 1961. (Jack Fisher, incidentally, had given up No. 60, and much was made of the coincidence when he joined Stallard on the Mets.)

Bunning's wife and one of their daughters had made the trip to New York to take in the World's Fair. Soon they—and the other six little Bunnings watching on TV at home—were caught up with the thousands of fans in the excitement of the moment. The Phillies were winning easily, but Jim Bunning, baseball's father of the year, was pitching a perfect game.

About the only man in the ball park who didn't show any emotion was Bunning, who had already pitched a no-hitter for Detroit in the American League. The tall, thin, and impossibly cool veteran remained in good humor as he mowed down the Mets. From the seventh inning on, he conducted his personal countdown in the dugout each time the Phils prepared to take the field. "Okay, you guys, you've only got to get me nine more outs," he exhorted his fielders. Then it was six more outs and three more outs, and finally John Stephenson, a rookie, struck out to provide Bunning with his perfect game and the 6-0 victory. At least something was perfect about the Mets.

*Down at Cocoa, Florida, a young Met left-hander was mak-
ing his pro debut in the Florida Rookie League. Tug McGraw
pitched a no-hitter.*

To coincide with the opening of Shea Stadium and the hoop-la
of the World's Fair, the Mets had been awarded the 1964 All-Star
Game. Players voted on the participants, and there was genuine
excitement in New York when it became apparent that Ron Hunt,
improving on his fine rookie year, might become the first Met ever
to make the team on his merits and start in an All-Star Game.

The pugnacious second-baseman won easily and received a tremendous ovation from the crowd of over 50,000 when he was
introduced before the game. "Eat your heart out," Hunt joked to
Joe Torre, who had been introduced just ahead of him, "but I play
here." Hunt contributed a base hit as the Nationals won, 7-4.

At the All-Star break, the Mets were in tenth place, and that's
where they remained for the rest of the season. Still, they did win
two more games than they had managed in any previous season.

This "greatest Met team ever" had three .300 hitters and three
pitchers who won in double figures: Jackson with eleven victories
and Stallard and Fisher with ten each. Stallard also lost twenty.
Hunt, of course, led the regulars with a .303 average and played
All-Star ball all year. Right-fielder Joe Christopher batted right at
.300 but his fielding was suspect. An introverted Virgin Islander,
Christopher did not mix with the other players, and they would
criticize him publicly for his fielding lapses. "The only .300 hitter
who hurts a team," Stallard once said after Christopher had cost
him a ball game. But Joe Christopher could wiggle his baseball cap
by controlling the muscles in his scalp, he was a gentleman, and
he sorely missed his family back in the Caribbean. He said he
became a .300 hitter thanks to some tips on batting in a booklet by
Hall-of-Famer Paul Waner he had bought for 75 cents during the
winter.

*About the time of Stallard's blast at Christopher, the Fourth
Army baseball tournament was beginning at Fort Bliss, Texas.
There would be a lot of scouts watching this competition. Red
Murff worked for hours to get the star Fort Bliss pitcher under
contract to the Mets before the other scouts could see him.*

He succeeded, but since Jerry Koosman was not yet twenty-one, his father had to wire approval of the contract from Appleton, Minnesota.

Cannizzaro was the third .300 hitter and posted a .311 in part-time duty. Cannizzaro had spent years rusting in the Cardinals' farm system, and it took a while for him to resharpen his old skills. This original expansion Met had a great arm, but as Stengel at first complained, "This Canzonari can throw, but he can't catch." By now, however, Cannizzaro had developed into a pretty good workman behind the plate. In four seasons with the Mets, he never hit a home run. He never hit close to .300 again, either, because this would be the only season during which Wes Westrum served as Met first-base coach.

Westrum was an expert at stealing signs. He could spot little mannerisms that would reveal whether the pitcher was going to throw a fast ball or a curve. Standing in the first-base coaching box, he could then signal the hitter. Cannizzaro could hit a fast ball if he knew it was coming. Not all Mets were completely beyond help.

The No. 1 Youth of America

The thrown baseball came whizzing in from the outfield, high over four or five outstretched gloves. It crashed through a window in the Mets' Saint Petersburg clubhouse and thudded against the wall in Casey Stengel's office, only a couple of feet from the manager's head. After a second, when he recovered his composure, Casey peered through the shattered glass to see whose fielding practice had just showed he needed a lot more work.

"It's that Su-boda." Stengel shrugged. "A good thing he didn't hit me 'cause if I was dead he'd be in Buffalo."

Stengel didn't mean that if he had been hit in the head, Ron Swoboda would have been sent to the minors as punishment. What he was saying in Stengelese was that he was the only member of the Mets' hierarchy who wanted to keep Swoboda around. Without Casey, the broad-shouldered outfielder would lose his only friend in court.

Met headquarters in New York was getting scouting reports on a skinny right-handed pitcher from Texas. One game in March he struck out thirteen batters even though he developed a blister on his middle finger. Blisters and other ailments would plague Nolan Ryan all the way to the big leagues.

Swoboda, called "Li'l Abner" by some and "Swug" by others and worse by less charitable teammates, was a big, raw, powerful, likable Saint Bernard with a Chinese step-grandfather. He had

71

played freshman ball at the University of Maryland and gave every indication he intended to remain in school to get his degree. However, after he enjoyed that big tournament in Johnstown, Pennsylvania, the Mets figured he might be ready to change his mind. In a conference around the Swobodas' kitchen table that lasted well into the night, it was agreed that Ron would turn professional with the Mets for a $35,000 bonus.

When Swoboda showed up at the 1964 "instructural school," he had never played a single inning as a professional, and it showed. However, his tremendous home-run power also showed. He had all the raw equipment. He didn't know how to hit, but when he connected balls flew "over buildings," according to Stengel. He would catch fly balls hit anywhere near him and drop few, but he didn't know how to field. He had a strong arm, but he didn't know how to throw.

Stengel kept Swoboda around as long as he could that first spring, and then Ron was sent to the minor-league training base, where his more sophisticated teammates called him "Dummy" for his various gaffes. But he managed to tie for the Eastern League home-run championship in his first year as a pro in pretty fast company. Perhaps he should have been started out in a much lower league where he would have had a chance to learn to play the game. Instead, Swoboda was thrown in over his head from the start and had to fight to keep from being embarrassed at the plate. This led to his famous lapses in the field.

However, the big guy stayed with it. "Nothing in baseball ever came easy for me, not even in Little League or in high school. I don't expect it to come easy for me now," he declared.

Stengel liked to talk about his Youth of America program. He knew these youngsters would be the salvation of the Mets, and years later they were. Swoboda was his first real dividend, an exciting potential star. Swoboda's first major-league hit was a pinch home run that flew over the visiting team's bullpen at Shea, and Houston players couldn't believe the ball had been hit that far. They thought somebody in the outfield had thrown it over.

Swoboda ended up hitting nineteen home runs his rookie year, but not one of them after August 26. Pitchers began to tease him at the plate and make him look foolish, and the rookie would go into fierce rages. Once, after striking out, he was stomping his batting helmet on the dugout floor and his spikes got caught and he

"Oldest and Ugliest": Yogi Berra (left) and Warren Spahn.

had to hop around for several minutes before he could get loose. Stengel benched him on the spot for that stunt. As his hitting slumped, Swoboda's fielding also suffered. One veteran muttered, "If the ball is ever hit to that kid for the third out and he's behind you, you'd better not start trotting in to the bench without looking because he's liable to think it's only two out and hit you in the back of the head when he throws the ball in."

But Stengel knew that Swoboda had the God-given gift of home-run power. He would learn the other things in time. Mickey Mantle had been Casey's monument with the Yankees. Time was running out on the old man. If he was to make a star with the Mets, it would have to be Swoboda.

While Swoboda represented the future, the Mets also tried to

The plays that made Swoboda famous: hitting with power,
playing a simple base hit into a triple.

reach back into the past by hiring two new coaches they hoped
might also make a contribution on the playing field. Yogi Berra,
the great catcher, who had been created as a buffoon by Stengel,
had been named manager of the Yankees the season before. He won
the pennant and carried the Cardinals to seven games in the World
Series before losing. But he didn't win with enough style. His
Yankee bosses thought Berra should have won with ease. Little did
they know that Berra had done a great job keeping the deteriorating
Yankee flagship afloat for one more season or that the Mets would
win a pennant before the Yankees won another one. Berra was
summarily dismissed by the Yankees, and the Mets quickly moved

to hire him. It was another public relations coup and it didn't hurt the ball club. Although he hid it well,* Berra was a wise baseball man. He tried a brief comeback as a player but gave it up after four games, even though he had managed two hits in nine trips and a lot of Mets were doing worse.

The Mets expected much more on the field from their second player-coach, Warren Spahn, but got less on both counts. Spahn, forty-four, was the greatest left-hander in baseball history, but he had overstayed his welcome with the Braves, who let him go for cash. The Braves had wanted Spahnie to try pitching relief, but his insistence on remaining a starter was hampering development of younger men, they felt.

Spahn's record meant everything to him. If he hadn't been so singleminded, he would have given in to past discouragements. The key to his greatness eventually led to his downfall. "I consider myself more a pitcher than a coach," Spahn proclaimed on his signing and, when somebody suggested that he and Berra might form baseball's oldest battery, he quipped, "Not only the oldest, but the ugliest."

The Spahn experience was a disaster. He spent the training period getting himself ready to open the season and, once the campaign began, concentrated on adding to his impressive record of victories. For some reason, he got down on Larry Bearnarth, the sensitive right-handed pitcher who had done so well in relief the last couple of years. Spahn ignored Bearnarth, who never got called into a game unless Stengel personally ordered it. Larry never recovered from the shattering experience.

Spahn ended up with a 4-and-12 record for the Mets, but with each start he was knocked out of the box earlier and earlier. Still, he stubbornly refused to take himself out of the regular rotation or pitch relief, which, Stengel felt, would both prolong his career and help the team. "What about my record?" Spahn asked during a closed-door argument with Stengel that could be heard out in the hall.

"Yeah, but what about mine?" Stengel countered bitingly.

* "Nobody goes to that restaurant any more, it's too crowded."

"How do you like your new house, Yogi?"
"It's full of rooms."

"My, you look cool on this warm day, Yogi."
"Yeah, and you don't look so hot yourself."

Within weeks, Spahn was fired as both pitcher and coach. Wes Westrum took over his duties. When Berra took over as first-base coach, where he would be in the public eye, Westrum moved to Stengel's right hand in the dugout.

While Spahn was still effective early in the season, a sophomore right-hander was compiling a 10-2 record for the Southern Cal baseball team. But only the Dodgers appeared to be interested in Tom Seaver.

There were also two moves of significance in the front office before the 1965 season. The championship St. Louis Cardinals had won their pennant under the same conditions as the Yankees had, with top management showing complete lack of confidence early in the season. Their owner also wanted to fire the manager, Johnny Keane, but Keane's close friend General Manager Bing Devine resigned instead. Eddie Stanky, Devine's chief aide, also quit, and both were snapped up by the Mets. (Keane also resigned after the season and, in one of the year's great ironies, moved over to the Yankees to succeed Berra.)

Devine was named assistant to the president, and there was every indication that he would succeed George Weiss the following year. Stanky was named director of player personnel, but he resigned after one season to become field manager of the White Sox. All through 1965, Stanky and Devine ranged through the bush leagues of America, revitalizing the Mets' scouting organization and minor-league farm system. It was during their travels that the groundwork was laid for the Mets' miracle of 1969. Hard work was the secret ingredient.

The University of Iowa lost an important Big Ten baseball game to Ohio State, but it was the losing pitcher, a skinny psychology major, who impressed Met scout Charley Frey. That June the Mets drafted Jim McAndrew.

Although the Mets' opening losing streak was only two games, the 1965 season was one of disappointment and injury, and once again the Mets finished tenth. With only fifty victories, they had their worst record since the first season. Two youths of America led the team in hitting, Ed Kranepool with a .253 average and Ron

Swoboda with nineteen home runs. But Al Jackson lost twenty games and Jack Fisher twenty-four.

Disaster, as usual, did not come without warning. The Mets hired former Olympic track star Jesse Owens to teach their players physical fitness in spring training, and Owens ended up hobbling with a back injury. The roll call of injuries was added to on successive days in May, less than a month after the opening of the season.

On the 10th, the Mets played their biennial exhibition game at West Point. The contest is preceded by a luncheon with the Corps of Cadets and other ceremonies, and Stengel was late getting dressed for the game. As he rummaged through his traveling bag, he saw that the clubhouse boy had neglected to pack his ripple-soled shoes and so he quickly donned a regular pair of baseball spikes. As he scurried up the concrete runway to the dugout, he slipped and broke his arm.

The injury to the seventy-four-year-old manager was minor, and he didn't miss a game, pointing out, "I don't manage with my wrist." But what happened to his twenty-four-year-old second-baseman the following night was really serious. In a basepath collision with the Cardinals' Phil Gagliano, Ron Hunt incurred a shoulder separation and had to undergo surgery. He was out until August 27.

It was indicative of the low estate of the Mets and their minor-league system that there was nobody else available to play second base.

Down at their Auburn, New York, farm, a young Texan was breaking into the pros by hitting safely in his first nineteen games. Ken Boswell ended up being named the New York–Penn League's Rookie of the Year.

George Weiss called frantically all over baseball seeking a replacement for Hunt, and about midnight he was able to purchase the Giants' Chuck Hiller. Hiller was known as "Iron Hands" because of his poor fielding. But he survived in the majors on a pretty good bat and a better sense of humor. He even had hit a World Series grand-slam home run for the Giants.

One day the Mets were anxious to get out of town after blowing a series in Chicago on a streak of demoralizing plays, including some damaging errors by Hiller. Gus Mauch, the old trainer Weiss

Wes Westrum posts his first lineup card
as interim manager of the Mets.

had brought with him from the Yankees, was berating the Mets on their lack of haste in getting dressed and packed. Soon he was involved in a screaming match with several of the disgruntled players. "It wasn't like this with the old Yankees," said Mauch, who shared with Weiss a love for those good old well-ordered days. "Why, Mickey Mantle was always the first one to have his bag packed."

From his corner stall, Hiller piped up, "Well, frazzle to Mickey Mantle . . . and frazzle to Joe DiMaggio, too."

This complete lack of respect for his idols silenced Mauch.

On another trip, to Milwaukee, the Mets sent Jesse Gonder across the hall to the Braves on a waiver deal, and the portly catcher couldn't wait to join his new club. "I'm not as bad a catcher as you —— think I am," he once had told the writers. Gonder also thought official scorers erred on the number of passed balls charged against him.

"You're right," countered Tracy Stallard, traded away to the

Cardinals before the '65 season. "A lot of them are called wild pitches."

Ironically, while Gonder was leaving the Mets, a catcher for the White Sox was setting a major-league record for passed balls with thirty-three. But J. C. Martin was catching a staff loaded with knuckleball pitchers.

The Mets were staging their Old-Timers' Day program on July 24, a Saturday, and that night they entertained all the old ballplayers at a party. The party ran late, very late, and Joe DeGregorio of the Met front office, who lived near Shea, volunteered to take Casey home so he wouldn't have so far to go the next morning for Sunday's doubleheader with the Phils.

As Stengel got out of DeGregorio's car, he slipped and fell to the sidewalk, but he didn't feel he was hurt badly and went on to bed. The next morning, he couldn't move. His hip was broken. Casey Stengel, who had laughed at his years for so long, finally had been felled by an old person's injury less than a week before his seventy-fifth birthday.

In the hospital, they asked Casey who he wanted to take charge of the team. "Westrum's the one," he replied.

9

Along Came Jones

On August 30, the Mets called a press conference. Casey Stengel, on the advice of his physician, was retiring from baseball. "How can I go out and change a pitcher when I need this?" Stengel growled as he brandished his new cane. Mrs. Payson said it all: "Casey made the Mets."

Wes Westrum was given the title of "interim manager."

In those closing weeks, Westrum dedicated himself to a youth movement, especially in the pitching department. Dick Selma got plenty of chances, and he struck out thirteen Milwaukee Braves in one game for a club record. And Tug McGraw, the wild-eyed and handsome left-hander whose early ambition was to be a barber, became the first Met ever to best the Dodgers' Sandy Koufax. Exhilarated by the experience, he leaped off the mound after the final out. His trouble was that he met adversity with just as violent a reaction. Control was Tug McGraw's problem, and not of his pitches.

Everyone but the Met owners was impressed by the job Westrum had done those final weeks. "Don't call us, we'll call you," they advised in essence as Wes packed his bags to return home to Phoenix for the winter. The season ended on October 3. For six miserable weeks Westrum was kept hanging in a state of agonizing limbo. They didn't fire him, they didn't drop him back to coach, they didn't make him manager. They waited.

The excuse was that Mrs. Payson was out of the country and no decision could be reached until her return. In reality, some of the directors wanted a big-name manager and kept holding out for such as Alvin Dark. Rather than bruise the feelings of a minority stockholder, whose vote could be overruled with ease, the Met management crucified Wes in slow stages. Finally, when a secret survey of fans proved to the balky director that Westrum's name was indeed recognizable around New York, Grant placed a phone call to Phoenix. At 9:15 A.M. Westrum picked up the receiver to hear Grant's jolly voice ask, "Hello. Is this the new manager of the New York Mets?"

So Westrum had to go out and buy his first tuxedo.

Westrum had started in baseball for Crookston, Minnesota, in the Northern League for $100 a month at seventeen years of age in 1940. His route to the majors had been tortuous and low-paying and was interrupted by army service in World War II.* He resented today's youngsters, who had made the same trip quickly and under first-class conditions, and this was to color his brief career as a manager. Crookston was a farm club of the Giants, and Wes finally made the parent team in 1949. He was their regular catcher for the famous 1951 pennant drive, when the Little Miracle of Coogan's Bluff was capped by Bobby Thomson's playoff homer against the Dodgers.

While the Giants were overhauling the Dodgers that September, Westrum suffered from several injured fingers. He couldn't grip a bat, but he could still catch. "I don't care if you never get a hit, I want you in there to handle my pitchers," manager Leo Durocher had told him. So Westrum caught every day, the Giants won the pennant, and he batted .219. After the season, Westrum felt that Durocher neglected to see that he was rewarded for the sacrifice of his batting average, and thus began a long and deep dislike.

Westrum helped the Giants win two National League pennants and one world championship. When he retired with a .217 lifetime average after the 1957 season, Giant owner Horace Stoneham said he intended to reward him for his loyal service. "I want you to stay on as a coach, but I don't ever want you to become the manager because that means someday I would have to fire you," Stoneham told him.

Westrum served as a coach with the Giants for six years. How-

---

* Prior to getting the Met job, Westrum's only managerial experience was with a service team. Wes was stationed at a disciplinary barracks and always stressed "not as an inmate."

ever, in 1961 Alvin Dark became manager of the Giants, and he and Westrum, former teammates, did not get along. Before the 1964 season, Dark succeeded in having Westrum transferred off his coaching staff and into scouting. This is where the coincidences began. Cookie Lavagetto, the Met coach, had been ill and expressed a desire to take a job nearer his home in Oakland, California. So he took Westrum's vacant spot with the Giants. Stoneham then tipped off the Mets that Westrum was available for a coaching assignment. It was announced as a "trade" of coaches and turned out to be the best break Westrum ever got.

Westrum was an astute inside-baseball man who went through life perpetually red-eyed, as if he'd just stopped weeping, a good demeanor for anyone associated with the Mets. He was an outstanding coach. When the players reported to Westrum's first training camp, they were greeted with a long list of suggestions on how to approach the game of baseball, plus a poem stressing positive thinking.

After losses, the Mets were enjoined to sit silently staring into their lockers for ten minutes to meditate on what they had done wrong. "Positive thinking" would be Westrum's watchword. "Positive thinking" would lift the Mets into the first division. Westrum wanted the Mets to start thinking big. When he was asked to predict how the Mets would do in their exhibition games, Westrum went right out on a limb. He said they'd win half of them.

On April 1, the Mets transacted a minor-league deal with the Cardinals, surrendering Danny Napoleon for Tony Martinez and Art Mahaffey, once a pretty good big-league pitcher. When Martinez reported with a dead arm, the Mets returned him and demanded another player. In mid-October the Cardinals finally delivered, a five-year minor-leaguer, infielder Bobby Pfeil.

The season of 1966 was dedicated to getting the Mets out of last place. George Weiss had been expected to retire as president at this point in favor of Bing Devine, but he elected to stay on the job one more year. He did not want to retire as a last-place president (or at all for that matter). Devine could wait. The Mets had been exciting, albeit losers, with youth near the end of 1965. This season they would play it safe with age. Veteran players like

Cleon Jones: He came of age.

Ken Boyer, Jack Hamilton, Al Luplow, Ed Bressoud (in a trade for Joe Christopher), and Dick Stuart and old pitchers like Bob Shaw, Bob Friend, and Ralph Terry were obtained through trade and purchase. The Mets would never win a pennant with these guys but maybe they could finish ninth.

The College World Series in Omaha is a double elimination tournament. Arizona State won in the minimum number of games, but before the final victory, State's star pitcher, Gary Gentry, told his coach he'd be willing to come back the next day without any rest if necessary.

Well, the Mets did finish ninth, but it was no big deal. The Chicago Cubs were busy tearing their team apart for new manager Leo Durocher, and they plummeted all the way to tenth. The Houston Astros still finished ahead of the Mets, in eighth. The Mets' season-opening losing streak was ended at one this year and, with sixty-six victories, this was easily "the greatest Met team of all time." The collapse would come later.

The season of 1966 would not really be remembered as the year the Mets climbed out of the cellar because it turned out to be such a tentative step. Of greater significance, it was the year Cleon Jones made it to the big leagues.

Cleon Jones, from a productive baseball nest around Mobile, Alabama, was one of the first free agents ever signed by the Mets their first season of 1962. He had been an all-round sports star in high school and went to Alabama A&M as a football player. He could have been a pro star in that sport, too, but he signed with the Mets and that winter started his career in the winter instructional league. There he produced glowing reports from manager Solly Hemus, who labeled him a potential superstar before Cleon had even played an inning in a real pro league. Hemus was the first to recognize the magnitude of Jones' potential, but it took several years for that potential to be realized.

It seemed that every year Jones would come to training camp all set to become a regular outfielder with the Mets. He had done well in the minors the year before and would do even better in the early weeks of spring training. The Mets wanted to keep him on their roster. Then something would go wrong. The first year, he blew his chance of making it right off the bat by foolishly delaying some minor surgery. In training camp for the 1964 season, he was thrown off stride by a bad reaction to the shots he had to take for the trip to Mexico. And in '65, it was bad teeth.

As they made plans for 1966, the Mets thought it might be wise to turn Cleon into a switch-hitter. He batted right-handed but was a natural lefty and did everything else left-handed, including throw. It seems that when he was a youngster, all the other kids batted right-handed and Cleon just thought that was the only way to do it. Since he hadn't developed into much of a pull-hitter, the Mets thought switch-hitting would make him an added threat. However, playing in Puerto Rico that winter, Jones suddenly developed into a pull-hitter. Met scouts saw and rushed back their reports. The switch-hitting experiment was wiped off the drawing board.

Later that spring Met plans in another direction were stymied. They wasted a draft choice on a skinny outfielder who just didn't think he was ready for pro ball. However, the next year Rod Gaspar would give the Mets permission to draft him again, and they did.

Jones came to the 1966 training camp as a new player and a new person. In previous years, his conversation seldom rose above a whisper and his gaze seldom rose above the floor. He was timid and shy and later he would confess, "I didn't feel like a major-leaguer." But this year he greeted friends with new confidence and he attacked pitchers with a new authority. He batted a robust .275, and he knew he had arrived when pitchers started knocking him down in the latter part of the season.

Cleon Jones was on his way and so were the Mets, at least to ninth place for one season. To make up for their previous cruelty, the Mets rewarded Westrum with a small raise and a new one-year contract on Labor Day. When the season ended with the Mets in ninth place, seven and a half games ahead of the Cubs, Westrum bought champagne.

10

The All-American

Under mild protest, with a minimum of kicking and screaming, George Weiss finally consented to retire after the 1966 season, and Bing Devine was elevated to the president's chair. Devine, through a series of astute trades, had turned the Cardinals into pennant contenders, and he quickly set out to do the same with the Mets. Weiss was conservative to a fault. Nobody would ever make the same accusation about Devine. Before the 1967 season had come to an end, the Mets would set major-league records by using twenty-seven different pitchers and fifty-four different players in all. The Mets would dazzle them with footwork if not with talent.

Within a month of taking office, Devine completed two major deals, one of which would have a profound, if delayed, effect on Met fortunes. He sent hero Ron Hunt, never exactly a hero to Manager Westrum, and Jim Hickman, last of the original Mets, to Los Angeles for Tommy Davis and Derrell Griffith; and he traded pitcher Dennis Ribant to Pittsburgh for Don Bosch and Don Cardwell.

Few noticed when the Mets drafted an all-round prospect from the Red Sox organization. Although Amos Otis had made the New York–Penn League All-Star team, Boston had not bothered to protect him.

The key men for the Mets in these trades were Tommy Davis and Don Bosch, both outfielders. Davis, a Brooklyn boy, had signed

They played better for Tom Seaver.

with the Dodgers because he wanted to play at home, and then they moved away on him. He won National League batting championships in 1962 and '63 and was one of baseball's most well-regarded young hitters until he broke his ankle in 1965. The injury almost ended his career. Even though Davis did come back to play the following season, Dodger Manager Walter Alston never regained confidence in him as a day-to-day player. He had never been an outstanding fielder before his injury, and now he was even slower. But he still could hit, a talent in short supply with the Mets. Griffith, an infielder, was traded along by the fast-moving Devine before the end of spring training, but Davis showed up Alston by playing 154 games for the Mets and batting .302. His big dividend would come later. Where the Mets were hurt in this deal was at second base, because rookie Ken Boswell, expected to take over for Hunt, went into the army.

While Devine was dealing, Met scouts were at work in the winter leagues. Nino Escalera liked what he saw of a Detroit prospect who was pitching in Puerto Rico. He thought the Mets might be able to use him. Two years later, in a minor-league deal, the Mets would give up catcher Hector Valle to get Jack DiLauro from the Tigers.

In Bosch, the Mets thought they had finally landed the center-fielder Casey Stengel had been seeking since 1962. Bosch had been named "Player of the Year" with the Pirates' Triple A farm team in Columbus, Ohio, and his manager, Larry Shepard, claimed, "he can cover as much ground as any center-fielder in baseball." However, cynics noted that Don Bosch, whom the Pirates said was so great, had been kept by them in the minor leagues for seven seasons.

Bosch was listed as 5-foot-10 and 160 pounds but on arrival in training camp appeared to be shorter and lighter. Worse, he didn't have it in him to carry the pressure of what the Mets expected. He was supposed to move right in and carry a major-league team, and he ended up unable to carry even his own glove. Nobody expected Bosch to be a great hitter right away, but writers in spring training were shocked when his fielding also appeared suspect. If it hadn't been for the spotlight trade, Bosch probably would have been cut in Florida. As it was, Westrum had to take him north and start him, but eventually Bosch was benched and sent to the minors. It may have been the worst trade Devine ever made, except that the throw-in, pitcher Don Cardwell, ended up winning twenty games in three years for the Mets and performed valuable duty the year of the pennant.

Partially obscured by Devine's season-long activity at the trading mart was the emergence of two more young products of the Met farm system.

Bud Harrelson, the shortstop Stengel had liked so much, was playing at Jacksonville early the year before when a handsome, broad-shouldered right-handed pitcher joined the team. Harrelson noticed right away how the team picked up whenever Tom Seaver pitched. "He seemed to expect so much of himself, and of all of us, and we responded," Harrelson would recall. He knew Seaver eventually would be giving the same lift to the Mets.

Harrelson was always interested in team motivation and all the little things that go into winning baseball. That's because Bud Harrelson was, and is, a little guy who needs to play all aspects of the game to succeed. He could appreciate and project the impact of a Tom Seaver because, unlike most ball players, he was aware of the organization picture beyond his own batting average. As an example, he never quibbled over any of his minor-league contracts. He figured he'd received his bonus, and until he made the majors, he actually represented a liability to the Mets.

The sharp-featured shortstop was signed out of San Francisco State in 1963 and didn't have much of a first year as a pro. In his thirty-sixth game for Salinas, he was hit on the arm with a pitch. The trainer "froze" it, and he trotted down to first base and finished the game. Later he learned it was broken. Out for the season. That winter Harrelson could have been drafted by any team in baseball for $8,000. However, a year later, the Mets had Harrelson tabbed as their shortstop of the future. His only problem was at the plate, and this was being solved in Jacksonville (which had replaced Buffalo as the Mets' top farm) as Harrelson worked at becoming a switch-hitter.

From the beginning, Seaver and Harrelson, both Californians, both strongly motivated young men, were friends. Seaver's father had been a tournament-class amateur golfer, and the achievement of sports excellence was always important in their family. Seaver grew up in Fresno, California, and played high school ball on the

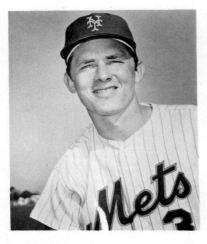

Bud Harrelson

Tommy Davis

Ken Boswell

Don Cardwell

same team as Dick Selma. "Even in high school, Tom knew all about setting up hitters. That's something I'm just learning," Selma would recall one day in admiration.

Seaver wasn't exactly a $40,000 pitching prospect from the beginning and, like the miracle Mets in 1969, he didn't spring from a cleft rock like the fictional Joe Hardy. As a senior in high school, Seaver was an unimpressive 5-foot-10, 155 pounds. But he went into the marines and came back three inches taller and 45 pounds heavier. He played a year at Fresno City College and then went to Southern Cal. In the summers he pitched for the Alaska Goldpanners, a strong semipro nine. Seaver had maturity (he was twenty-one) and a strong baseball background when the Mets signed him, which is why he was able to start out successfully at Triple A. Handsome and articulate, Seaver was the All-American boy with none of that gee-whiz, golly, soda-pop gush. Typical of many of today's new breed of young athletes, Seaver was aware of life beyond the foul lines.

Tom was 12-and-12 with Jacksonville in his first pro season, and the next spring he and Harrelson (who had preceded him by a couple of months when Roy McMillan was hurt) mounted their assault on Mt. Met Lethargy.

It was the same with the Mets as it was in Jacksonville. The team played better when Tom was pitching. He noticed this again, and it made him angry. If they were capable of playing well for him, why couldn't they do it for the other pitchers? It angered him to see professionals perform at less than their best. Unfortunately, few people in this world can fuel themselves with self-motivation. Not many could honestly answer "myself" as Tom Seaver did when asked to name his greatest influence in baseball. It hurt Seaver's pride to hear people laugh at the Mets, but at least he would never surrender to their image. If anything, he would make them over into his mold. This young pitcher they called "another Robin Roberts" won sixteen games, pitched in the All-Star Game, and became the first pitcher in a decade to be named National League Rookie of the Year.

For the second straight year, the Mets were able to limit their season-opening losing streak to one, but except for a few bright spots provided by Seaver, and Harrelson after a shaky start, things quickly deteriorated. The discipline Westrum had stressed in his pre-season pronouncements fell apart, and the team was back on its treadmill to oblivion.

"Oh, my God, wasn't that awful?" became Westrum's daily refrain. The team, once so colorful under Stengel, was lapsing into miserable dullness under Westrum.

The Mets' Williamsport farm club was en route through Connecticut by bus to play a road game when one of the players was taken violently ill. A catcher, he had been hit in the head by a bat the night before just three weeks after being kicked in the head during a play on the bases. Duffy Dyer was taken to a New Haven hospital and later given a complete neurological checkup. The Mets for a while feared he'd never play again.

Wes, an insecure man to begin with, saw no happy haven as the end of his second one-year contract drew nearer, especially when he recalled the reluctance to give him the job in the first place. The frustrations of losing and the insecurity tore at his insides and made him ill at night. There was no comfort in the manager's suite.

Everything was going wrong. Cleon Jones had followed his fine rookie year with a dismal slump that saw him batting under .200 until late June as Westrum criticized his lack of alertness. Attempts to "wake up" Ron Swoboda by making him a first-baseman had failed, and he still pulled stunts like locking himself in the batting cage. Tommy Davis hit his .302 and led his team in virtually every batting department, but otherwise was a very limited ballplayer. Ken Boswell was in the army, and catcher Jerry Grote was feeding Westrum's ulcer with his tantrums behind the plate.

Grote was another youngster whom expansion had rocketed into the majors ahead of schedule. In his second year as a pro, Grote was Houston's No. 1 catcher, but he hit only .181 and the next season was sent back to the minors. The Mets got him in a deal after the '65 season.

Grote had two problems, a stubbornness in calling pitches and a tendency to argue with umpires. Westrum, a former classic catcher himself, spotted every flaw. He probably would not have been as harsh on Grote if he had played another position. As the 1967 season progressed, Grote's temper and batting average both grew shorter.

The whole season seemed to be summed up in one night game in Los Angeles on July 27. Trailing, 3-2, after six innings, the Mets staged a minor rally in the seventh. John Sullivan, who was catching, got a single, and Westrum called on Grote to run for him. Then, later in the inning, Wes used his other catcher, Greg Goossen, as a pinch-hitter and then removed him from the game when the Mets took the field. This meant that Grote was now the only Met catcher left eligible to play. It was a good time for Grote to mind his manners, but in that very inning his neck reddened over a call by the umpire and the argument began. For the rest of the inning, Grote continued a running battle with the plate umpire. There is nothing an umpire hates more than to be shown up by a catcher and, as the eighth inning began, Grote continued yelling from the dugout and threw a towel. That was it. He was out of the game. The mortified Westrum had to seek volunteers to go behind the plate. Tommie Reynolds, an outfielder, was fitted into the protective tools to finish the game.

The incident still might have escaped becoming a *cause célèbre* if the Mets had remained supine and lost on schedule. But they rallied in the top of the eighth for a 5-3 lead, and now it was up to Tommie Reynolds to hold them. He couldn't. His passed ball let in the tying run in the eighth and the Dodgers won it in the eleventh, 7-6. Westrum fined Grote $100 for his tantrum, and Bing Devine called the young man the next morning from New York, to deliver a stinging lecture himself.

But Grote wasn't the only goat. Fault was found with Westrum, too. Why had he used up all his catchers in one inning? Why was he unable to control his players on the bench?

The season was drawing to a close. The Mets would lose 101 games in their slide back to tenth place, but there was still another figure that put Westrum's future in even greater jeopardy. Every season since 1962, the Mets had shown an increase in attendance. This year, for the first time, they not only would fail to show an increase, they would register their first drop at the gate. Was the golden goose laying sterile eggs? Attendance would still be sensational for a last-place team, over 1,500,000, but this was a decrease of over 350,000 from the previous season. The first downward dip of a sales graph has caused more than one corporate crisis, and it was no different with the Mets.

For weeks, Westrum sought some reassurance from his superiors concerning his future. Odds were he'd be fired at the end of the season. At best, he might expect a grudging one-year extension, which would only mean he'd have to go through the same thing all over again. On September 19, Wes Westrum composed a handwritten letter of resignation to Bing Devine. There is no record that anyone tried to talk him out of it.

As the Mets played out the season under the direction of coach Salty Parker, it was no secret whom they wanted to take over in 1968. Down in Washington, Gil Hodges had completed his apprenticeship. It was time for Gil to come home, but under baseball canon tampering with a man under contract is a major crime. Negotiations took on an aspect of intrigue. Johnny Murphy, Devine's top aide, and George Selkirk, general manager of the Senators, had been roommates as players with the Yankees. Using this personal contact, Murphy ascertained that the Senators would not stand in Gil's way. An official request was made to dicker with Hodges while Murphy and Selkirk settled on compensations for the Senators.

The deal with the Senators was made at a concession stand in St. Louis during the Cardinal–Red Sox World Series. For $100,000 and right-handed pitcher Bill Denehy, the Senators would give the Mets the right to sign Gil Hodges as manager. Gil was then introduced to Devine, for the first time, surprisingly, and they worked out the major clauses of his three-year contract on the drive to the airport.

Cries of "wife stealing!" greeted the news in Washington, where Hodges had become a popular figure. Many were surprised at how freely the Senators gave up their manager; some saw hidden motives. Apparently, it was just a good deed. The Senators knew that if they asked Gil to stay, he would. He owed them as much for giving him his first managerial job as they owed him for building their ball club. They knew Gil would not take any initiative in leaving. So they gave him a little nudge in the direction they knew he wanted to take: back home.

When Gil Hodges became the new manager of the Mets, he was, in a sense, their first complete manager. Stengel had been hired for his appeal as much as his ability on the field. Except for veto power, he didn't even pick his own coaches. Weiss did that, and they provided an ever-changing platoon. Westrum had some say on coaches but operated on a tenuous year-to-year deal that undermined his authority. Except for Yogi Berra, a fixture, Hodges was able to bring in his own staff and he operated from a position of strength with his three-year contract. When he called his players together the following spring and spelled out his demands, Tom Seaver had to know his campaign to bring excellence to the Mets would no longer be a one-man job.

Gil

Funny thing about Gil Hodges. It's as if he was born the day he put on a Brooklyn Dodger uniform. Maybe he was.

"It is like coming home," he confessed in a rare moment of self-revelation one afternoon soon after the Mets brought him back from Los Angeles in the expansion draft. "I wasn't much more than sixteen when I went away to college, and then I went into the marines. I don't guess I really had a home until I got to Brooklyn."

Even in his book, a combination autobiography and instructional guide, Hodges ignores his early life. And the omission is even more striking because the book is aimed at managers of little-league teams, and Hodges' early experiences would have been most pertinent. There seems to have been nothing unusual about Hodges' early life, and he remains close to his family. But to Gil, a private life is private. Why this extreme reticence? Gil hides the clues.

The record shows Gilbert Raymond Hodges was born with the 1924 baseball season, on April 4, in Princeton, Indiana, a small coal-mining town in the southwest corner of the state, not far from Evansville. Gil's father was a miner, and he and his brothers helped out by working in the tool sheds of the mining company. That's where Gil, who grew up to be a 6-foot-2 200-pounder, got all those muscles. "He could squeeze your ear-brows off," Casey Stengel once breathed in awe.

After high school, where he participated in most sports, Gil left home for St. Joseph's College in Rensselaer, Indiana, about 200 miles away. After a couple of years of college he was spotted as a shortstop by a Dodger scout named Stan Feezle. This was 1943 and there was a war on. Most big-league organizations were cutting back on their operations. Why sign a kid who was ready to go into the army? But Branch Rickey, as always, was ahead of them. He knew the war would be over one day. He directed his Dodger scouts to increase their activity. "Sign everybody," he ordered. As usual, Rickey was right. When the war ended, all his young men returned to civilian life en masse. He had a huge corner on talent. This was how the Dodger dynasty was born.

Following a tryout camp at Olean, New York, young Hodges was signed to a Dodger contract. His bonus called for a $500 payment immediately, another $500 when he got back from service. While awaiting his call by the marines, Hodges finished out the 1943 season with the parent Dodgers. During those wartime years, almost anyone with two arms and two legs could qualify as a major-leaguer, and sometimes even these requirements were waived.

A catcher and a shortstop in college, Hodges played in only one game for the 1943 Dodgers . . . at third base. He struck out twice against Cincinnati's Johnny VanderMeer and committed two errors. His most vivid memory, though, is his first road trip. The traveling secretary stupidly paired this teen-age rookie with one of the team's veterans, a notorious carouser. As he was awakened every night by the old-timer stumbling into bed after curfew, young Gil could only wonder, This is the big leagues?

After his one game with the Dodgers, Gil went into the marines, where he became something of a legend in the Pacific theater of operations. "We'd keep hearing about this big guy from Indiana who went around killing Japs with his bare hands," Don Hoak, another marine who later played with the Dodgers, used to relate. After two and a half years in the service, Hodges returned to civilian life for his one and only season in the minors with Newport News, Virginia, of the Piedmont League. Hodges was the catcher. First base belonged to a big guy named Chuck Connors, who eventually did better in television.

Because of a special rule to protect former servicemen, Gil had to be brought up to the Dodgers in 1947, and he spent most of the season on the bench. He appeared in only twenty-eight games as Brooklyn won the pennant, and he struck out as a pinch-hitter his only time at bat in the World Series.

The following year, 1948, provided the two big changes in

Hodges' young life as he became established as a big-league ball player and sank his roots forever in the borough of Brooklyn. On the field, he was shifted from catcher to first base, where he quickly became a standout regular. After the season he married the former Joan Lombardi, and they settled down to live happily ever after in the bride's home borough of Brooklyn.

It took a series of interlocking events for Hodges to become a first-baseman. In 1947, Jackie Robinson played the position, with Bruce Edwards catching and Eddie Stanky on second base. After the season, Rickey traded Stanky to the Braves so Robinson could be moved over to second. When the 1948 season opened, Preston Ward was the Dodger first-baseman. Edwards had a sore arm, and so Hodges was the catcher. During these early weeks, however, Ward went into a batting slump, and down on the Dodgers' St. Paul farm club, Roy Campanella was showing that he deserved to be catching in the big leagues. In May, Leo Durocher, the Dodger manager, suggested that Gil start working out at first base. The following month the shift was made official. Hodges began his brilliant career at first as Campanella was called up from St. Paul to catch. Campy deserved getting precedence behind the plate. He made the Hall of Fame.

The Dodgers finished third in 1948 as Boston, led by the discard, Stanky, won the pennant. But Brooklyn eagerly awaited "next year." With the midseason player shifts, Rickey and Durocher had welded a team that would win six pennants and show three seconds in the next eleven years. Hodges, Robinson, Reese, Cox, Campanella, Furillo, Snider, Hermanski. This was the basic lineup that would become one of the great teams in baseball history with an incredible balance of offense and defense.

For ten years, Gil's idyl was uninterrupted. The Dodgers won pennants in 1949, 1952, 1953, 1955, and 1956. When they beat the Yankees in 1955, it marked Brooklyn's first world championship. And on August 31, 1950, against the Braves, Hodges established himself as one of baseball's premier sluggers when he became only the sixth man ever to hit four home runs in a single game.

Even in adversity things were good, as Hodges was in the happy position of playing among his friends and neighbors. When the Dodgers lost the 1952 World Series to the Yankees in seven games, Gil Hodges did not get a single base hit in twenty-one times at bat. But far from booing their hero, fans gave him an inspiring ovation every time he walked up to the plate. (On another occasion, when Hodges was in a slump, a priest was celebrating Mass in a Brooklyn school. "It's too hot today for a sermon. Go home, keep the Commandments—and say a prayer for Gil Hodges," the priest told his youngsters. Then, as now, religion was an important part of Gil's life.)

After the 1957 season, however, the world of Gil Hodges suffered a traumatic shock. The Dodgers were moving to Los Angeles. Hodges, only thirty-four and with a lot of baseball still to play, had to go along. But his home remained in Brooklyn and, despite another pennant and world championship, it was not a happy time.

Then, in October of 1961, came the word. The Mets had spoken and Gil Hodges was coming home.

Met fans greeted the news with great joy, but the homecoming was not much more than symbolic. Opening day of 1962 was a week after Gil's thirty-eighth birthday. He was baseball old and he had a bad knee. Still, he hit the Mets' first home run ever in the 11-4 opening-day loss to St. Louis, and he managed to play in fifty-three more games and hit eight more home runs the rest of the year. Casey Stengel never forgot the sore-legged old veteran's effort for his sagging last-place team.

During the off-season, Hodges underwent knee surgery, but when he tried to come back the next season, his leg couldn't make it. After eleven games, he went on the disabled list, his seventeen-year career at an end. He had hit 370 home runs, at that time the most ever in the National League by a right-handed batter, and he had been named eight times to play in the All-Star Game. His fourteen grand-slam home runs were a league record. He was acknowledged as one of the finest fielding first-basemen of all time.

More important, he was totally respected by fans, teammates, and opponents. Even umpires. He had never been thrown out of a game for arguing with an umpire, and nobody could remember this gentle giant of a man ever being involved in a fight on the field, except for one time when the Dodgers and Cubs were involved in a brawl and Hodges could be seen astride the squirming mass of bodies, picking them up one by one and throwing them aside like a housewife sorting wash.

There was little time for Hodges to rest at home and run his bowling alley, however. The Washington Senators of the American League were looking for a manager, and their front-office boss, George Selkirk, held a couple of secret meetings in New York with the now-former first-baseman. When they saw discussions might reach the serious stage, Selkirk approached the Mets for permission to negotiate with Hodges. And on May 22, 1963, Mickey Vernon was let out as manager of the Senators and Hodges was named to replace him. For the rights to Hodges, who was still Met property, the Senators had to surrender outfielder Jim Piersall.

> *While negotiations were under way between Hodges, the Mets, and the Senators, talks of a different nature were going on in California involving a spindly shortstop at San Francisco State College. The Yankees wanted him, but he turned them down because their lineup appeared set for many years. The Cardinals wanted to send him up to a semipro league in Alaska. Met Scout Roy Partee knew he had to talk and act fast. He did. On June 7, 1963, the Mets signed Bud Harrelson for a bonus of just over $11,000. That same day, Harrelson filled out a personal questionnaire for the club. "The hardest thing to do in baseball?" it asked. "Keeping the entire team hustling," the nineteen-year-old rookie replied.*

Hodges performed no immediate miracles after he took over the Senators from Vernon. The team was tenth and it finished tenth. But Gil was learning his trade—and in a new league after a lifetime in the National.

The education of Gil Hodges continued through the 1964 season, and the Senators improved to ninth place with twenty-two more victories than they had posted the year before. Hodges began to get a reputation as a disciplinarian. He was tough. He made the rules and the Senators lived by them. When one of his players, who had been fined several times for missing curfew, came to him one night for special permission to stay out late for some reason or another, Hodges replied softly, "I don't care if you stay out, and stay out, and stay out, and never come back." The player made the curfew.

"It's a weird feeling being chewed out by Hodges. He never raises his voice and he never curses. It's like being chewed out by a computer," another player once recalled.

Yet Hodges had, and has, a temper, and it can explode, usually in private. With the press, he often showed a sarcastic humor capable of drawing blood if not inflicting permanent damage. In a public job, Hodges fulfilled all his obligations, but he still remained very much the self-contained private man—his personal feelings always hooded, all but the closest friends held away by a shield of reserve. Completely self-sufficient, Gil gave the impression the whole world could disappear and he'd never miss it.

As Steve Jacobson wrote in *Newsday* after-the Mets' World Series victory: "In the midst of all that incredible gaiety of the celebrating Mets I wish I had seen Gil Hodges just once let himself fall into a peal of laughter or weep for the joy of the moment. . . . I would have been pleased to have any evidence of emotion from Gil, but it wasn't coming—not excitement, not thanksgiving or even relief. . . . That's not Hodges' style."

By the end of his first full season with Washington, Hodges was in command of his new job. The Senators went to the winter baseball meetings and Hodges was confident enough to voice strong opinions on the personnel of his ball club. It was acknowledged that he was the main force behind the biggest trade in the Senators' brief history. Using his long association with Dodger general manager Buzzie Bavasi, Hodges was able to obtain massive outfielder Frank Howard, infielders Dick Nen and Ken McMullen, and pitchers Phil Ortega and Pete Richert in exchange for pitcher Claude Osteen and infielder John Kennedy. It was a master deal. It shored up the Senators in several positions and provided a slugger, Howard, who would become a superstar. The way Gil took charge signaled to those in the Senator family that he had arrived.*

With the aid of these new players, the Senators moved up to eighth in 1965. Late in that season, though, Hodges had cause to look north to his old team, the Mets. Casey Stengel slipped and broke his hip and Wes Westrum, a coach, was named interim manager. From the day he had first been picked in the expansion draft, many anticipated that Hodges would eventually manage the Mets. Now the job had opened up. Discussions through intermediaries were carried on through late summer. Hodges insisted that he never was personally approached about the job, and this was true. And the Mets never did get far enough to request permission to dicker with their old hero. Hodges reminded all who asked that he still had another year to go on his contract.

Meanwhile, Westrum was doing an impressive job subbing for Stengel, and the "interim" was removed from his title before the 1966 season. Down in Washington, the Senators finished eighth once again, while Westrum's Mets finally climbed out of the cellar for the first time in their five-year history and finished ninth. Westrum had earned another season as manager, and Hodges, with

---

* Bavasi, of course, was not exactly being a philanthropist. The two players he obtained, especially Osteen, helped him win two straight pennants.

no apparent regrets, signed a new two-year contract to pilot the Senators.

After all, the Mets were still a pretty poor ball club, he still had a lot to learn about managing, and besides, Washington was only a short train ride from Brooklyn.

12

The Year of the Farmer

The 1968 season started out the same as every other season for the Mets: they lost their opening game. The loss was like all the others, too. With Tom Seaver pitching, they jumped out, 4-0, against the Giants in San Francisco and then blew a two-run lead in the last of the ninth to lose, 5-4. Ho-hum.

Opening on the road provided one advantage for the Mets. It gave them a chance to play and lose a home opener, too, and in their first five years they had done just that. Jerry Koosman, a sharp-faced rookie left-hander who had already shut out the Dodgers in Los Angeles on the opening road trip, was given the dubious honor of pitching in the 1968 home inaugural.

His opponents at Shea were the Giants, a free-swinging bunch of sluggers led by Willie Mays, Jim Ray Hart, and Willie McCovey. Koosman's moment of truth began almost before the last notes of the "Star-Spangled Banner" had finished drifting out into Flushing Bay. Ron Hunt, the ex-Met, led off with a single, Jim Davenport reached base on an error, and Willie McCovey walked. Bases loaded, nobody out, and right-handed-hitting Willie Mays coming to bat in his favorite ball park. All the ingredients of disaster were in place.

Koosman had been up briefly with the Mets at the start of the previous season, and Mays had hit a home run off him on a low fast ball. Jerry's major concern was not to give Willie another pitch like that one. Working the veteran slugger like a master, Koosman struck him out. Hart was the next batter and he popped up, the runners holding. And then Koosman struck out Jack Hiatt as more than 50,000 fans exploded with a roar of approval . . . and relief. They had a new hero.

Koosman, who went on that afternoon to hold the Giants scoreless in becoming the first Met ever to pitch two consecutive shutouts, came into baseball under most unheroic circumstances.

His high school in the farming country around Appleton, Minnesota, didn't even have a baseball team, and Jerry used to rely on the informal "beer leagues" around home for his social and athletic outlet. During the winter he and his brother would work out evenings in their barn. Jerry began as the catcher, but when he started throwing the ball back harder than his brother, they reversed roles. Then the army called, and Jerry started at Fort Bliss, Texas, toward his rendezvous with Willie Mays.

Koosman's catcher on the Fort Bliss post team was a young New Yorker named John Lucchese, whose father worked as an usher at the Polo Grounds. One day John wrote his father, "We've got a pitcher down here the Mets could really use." The elder Lucchese turned his son's letter over to Joe McDonald, director of the Mets' minor-league operations, and McDonald forwarded the report to Red Murff, his Texas scout.

As the season of 1964 began, Murff went out to look at the young soldier. He liked his fast ball and his courage, but noted Koosman's "carefree" attitude and pointed out that post competition wasn't really the best. But he figured the kid was worth a shot and the sooner he was signed before too many other scouts saw him, the cheaper he'd come. Getting approval from the front office, Murff offered Jerry $1,600 to sign. Koosman turned him down. The next time they talked, Murff dropped his offer to $1,500. Again Koosman declined. With each visit, Murff lowered the ante by another $100. When he reached $1,200, Koosman capitulated. "I figured I'd better sign before I ended up owing them money," he confessed later.

At first the Mets feared they had overpaid him. In his rookie season of 1965, Koosman showed a losing record with two minor-league teams. Then, en route to spring training in '66, he stopped for a lark with a couple of other "carefree" young prospects and demolished his car in an accident somewhere in Georgia.

Late that night, McDonald received a frantic phone call at the Mets' minor-league complex in Homestead, Florida. "You gotta

Jerry Koosman proved himself against Willie Mays.

send me $75 right away or I'll never get out of here," Koosman pleaded.

Baseball clubs as a matter of policy do not advance money to such tentative prospects as Koosman during spring training. Players, even in the majors, are not on salary during this period, and with youngsters like Koosman there's a 50-50 chance they'll be released in spring training before they ever draw a paycheck and have a chance to reimburse the club. McDonald was reluctant, but Koosman sounded so desperate he decided to go out on a limb and wire him the money.

For a while, it looked as if the Mets were out $1,275 on Koosman. In the early weeks of training camp he showed nothing, and one night the assembled scouts and minor-league managers and coaches met to decide which players should be released as hopeless. Koosman's name came up. Few had anything encouraging to say before they took a vote. "Should Jerry Koosman be released?" Every hand in the room went up in assent . . . except one. "You can't release him, he still owes us $75," blurted McDonald, whose name was on the voucher.

And so for $75—McDonald says today he was no genius at spotting talent, the money was the only consideration—Jerry Koosman got another chance.

Kooz did a little better as camp progressed and was assigned to Auburn, New York, of the New York–Penn League. After missing the team flight north from Homestead—a now-typical gaffe that added another $16.01 (for a more expensive plane ride) to the $75 on his account—Kooz enjoyed an outstanding season with a league-leading 1.38 earned-run average. The next year, after coming north with the Mets, he won the International League strikeout title at Jacksonville. A winter in the instructional league and Jerry Koosman was ready for the majors—and Willie Mays.

The slider was the pitch that made Koosman a major-leaguer, but in the backward pattern of his baseball life it was the elimination of this pitch, rather than its addition, that turned the trick. Wes Stock, the Mets' minor-league pitching coach, started to make Koosman delete the pitch from his repertoire in the winter league. Then Rube Walker, the Mets' portly major-league pitching maestro, completed the task in spring training. Koosman simply did not throw the slider very well, but he did have the rudiments of an excellent curve. Eliminating the slider forced him to practice his curve and he now has a dandy to go with the outstanding fast ball he first developed in the barn in Minnesota.

Koosman, of course, wasn't the only new Met. The farm system was now producing, and the energetic Bing Devine was still trading. When he ran out of players to trade, he ended up trading himself. Although he had been employed by the Mets since 1964, Devine had never really left St. Louis. When he wasn't on the road for the ball club, he lived in a midtown Manhattan hotel. His family remained in St. Louis except for one summer when they came East and decided they didn't like it. When August (Gussie) Busch, owner of the Cardinals, decided that to forgive was Devine and asked Bing to come back home as general manager around Christmastime, the slender and dynamic baseball executive quickly accepted. Johnny Murphy, who had been with the Mets from the beginning, was named to succeed him.

Devine kept dealing for the Mets almost until his plane left for St. Louis. He retrieved Al Jackson (an original Met) from St. Louis and shuffled Bob Johnson, whom he had obtained only the season before, on to Cincinnati for a sideburned slugger named Art Shamsky. J. C. Martin, a catcher, was picked up from the White Sox as deferred payment for Ken Boyer, who had been dispatched to Chicago during the previous pennant race. And then Devine initiated conversations (later completed by Murphy) for the swap that would enable him to leave the Mets a pennant legacy.

In a five-player deal, he sent Tommy Davis, the outfielder he had obtained for Ron Hunt the year before, and pitchers Jack Fisher and Billy Wynne to the White Sox for center-fielder Tommie Agee and infielder Al Weis. The trade, in which he gave up a .300 hitter, Davis, and an established pitcher, Fisher, was a tremendous gamble that took two years to pay off.

Devine did not make this deal without support, however. With Don Bosch conceded as a failure, the Mets still had that gaping hole in center field. Even when Hodges was managing in Washington, he had been enamored of Agee and had tried to get him to play center field for the Senators. He urged Devine to deal for Agee if he could, and also recommended they try to get Weis.

Weis had missed half the previous season because of a knee injury incurred when he collided with the Orioles' Frank Robinson at second base. He had undergone surgery, but proved he was sound by playing for Chicago's winter instructional-league team. Hodges knew this quiet thirty-one-year-old Long Islander could do a standout job at any of the infield positions. With most of the Mets' young infielders facing weekend and two-week reserve calls during the summer, the Mets required a versatile veteran to fill in for them. Too, the regular shortstop, Bud Harrelson, had also undergone knee surgery that fall. Although he showed a certain degree of recovery by doing a mean twist with his wife at a baseball writers' party in December, he was still somewhat of a question. Weis could be the regular shortstop if necessary. Nobody expected him to hit, and they soon learned not to expect much in the way of long-winded conversation, either.

Agee, signed originally by the Indians, was traded to the White Sox while still a minor-leaguer and played his first full season in the majors in 1966. He broke in in spectacular fashion and was named American League Rookie of the Year with such credentials as a .273 average, twenty-two home runs, and forty-four stolen bases. He also led the league in several important fielding departments and seemed assured of a long and happy stay on Chicago's South Side.

But the next season his production fell off, and the White Sox became unhappy with their fine young prospect as his average dropped to .234 and his home runs to fourteen. Agee is a bachelor, and the White Sox thought he might have been enjoying too much night life. So they put a detective on his trail. As one of eleven children, Agee valued his privacy, and his performance wasn't helped by this lack of managerial confidence.

Agee's debut with the Mets was almost as dismal as that of his predecessor, the unfortunate Don Bosch. His first time up in an exhibition game, Agee was welcomed to the National League by being beaned by Bob Gibson. Through all the season, he never fully recovered emotionally from the impact of that blow, and at one point he tied Don Zimmer's Met record of going hitless in thirty-four straight times at bat. In one twenty-four-inning 1-0 loss in Houston, he went 0-for-10. His fielding fell off, too, and he managed no better than a miserly .217 average with only five home runs and seventeen runs batted in. Still, through it all, Agee kept hustling, kept trying to find ways to contribute, and his fans, teammates, and manager kept faith with him. Whenever he did achieve something at bat, he received a tremendous ovation. He would repay them all, he vowed.

The nucleus of a good ball club began to take form in 1968. Tom Seaver, after a poor start, won sixteen games for the second straight year, and Koosman won nineteen as he tied a National League rookie record with seven shutouts. He was runner-up in voting for National League Rookie of the Year, and both he and Seaver pitched in the All-Star Game.

In the outfield, Agee, despite his miseries, was encamped as Hodges' center-fielder and, in left, Cleon Jones seemed to get a tremendous lift from playing with Agee, a close friend and former high school teammate, and had his biggest year with a .297 average and fourteen home runs. In right field, the Mets got a combined twenty-three home runs from Ron Swoboda (eleven) and Art Shamsky (twelve).

Around the infield, Ed Kranepool continued to do a job of sorts at first base and Harrelson showed a full recovery at short. The two new emerging regulars were young Ken Boswell at second and old Ed Charles at third.

Back from his army hitch, Boswell continued to have his problems as a rookie. After getting off to a fine start, the young Texan broke his finger in June and played in only seventy-five games all year. But he batted .261, and the Mets were confident he would do even better.

Boswell's signing provided another example of how Met "luck," as in the Seaver case, was really what Branch Rickey liked to call "the residue of design." Boswell had been heavily scouted in high school, but his family wanted him to attend college and he enrolled at Sam Houston State in Huntsville, Texas. However, he was no scholar and he dearly wanted to play pro ball. When warm weather came, Boswell's thoughts began to wander from his books. Without apparent struggle, he flunked out of college.

The Mets, however, were the only organization aware of Boswell's scholastic indifference and his impending failure. As a college student, he could not be drafted. But what if he flunked out? The draft was on June 8. Boswell actually flunked out on the sixth, and the Mets got their ruling that same afternoon. Boswell could be drafted, and the Mets nabbed him on the fourth round as the competition cried.

"I always wanted to be a big-leaguer," Boswell said as he signed for a minimal four-figure bonus. "I'll never forget how, when I was fifteen, a scout from the White Sox told me he liked the way I played but for me to go home and grow."

Now, at age twenty-two and a solid 6-footer, Boswell was making it on all counts.

Charles' future was behind him when he was purchased by the Mets early in the 1967 season as another in their long line of third-basemen. He was thirty-four at the time and had been a pro since 1952. But given his rest, he could still field his position with such aplomb that his teammates called him "The Glider," and he still knew how to swing the bat with authority. Even when not playing, he was a tremendous addition to this essentially young team. A sensitive, gentle man, he wrote poetry in his spare time, and some of it had been published. After the 1967 season, the Mets had declared Charles a free agent, but he came to camp the next spring and won himself a spot on the roster all over again. With a team high of fifteen home runs, he proved there was still plenty of ride left in The Glider.

One of the big success stories of 1968 concerned Jerry Grote, the catcher who had seemed so far off the right track in 1967 when he batted only .195 under Westrum's lash. Even after his first training camp under Hodges, Grote was not the Mets' top catcher, and J. C. Martin won the honor of opening the season. However, in that initial game, Martin suffered a broken finger and had to be placed on the disabled list. Grote moved in and refused to be dislodged. He caught 30 of the next 31 games and 124 in all, batted a career high of .282, and was voted the National League's starting All-Star catcher. "All those bloop hits that never fell in for me before are falling in now," Grote would say in explaining his near 100-point rise, but he also conceded that a late spring batting tip from Hodges had been pretty important, too.

Still, the nucleus had not gelled into a team and the Mets, while avoiding tenth place for all but one day after the early weeks of the season, found themselves still faced with a possible last-place finish as the campaign drew to a close. This, Met brass felt, must be avoided at all cost. Over the grumblings of Rube Walker, the Friar Tuck of a pitching coach who nursed his young starters as if they were his own sons and who insisted on a five-day rotation, Koosman and Seaver were moved up as starters in the final two days.

The Mets, for the first time in their history, had a chance to finish ahead of Houston, and they didn't want to muff it. The Houstons had always been a pain to the Mets, a reminder for many years of their failure to be at least competitive, even from the days in dingy, dimly lit Colt Stadium. "If they're going to play night ball there, at least they should put in lights," Richie Ashburn said as he cursed the mosquitoes. Until the team moved into the Astrodome, Houston had the only ball park in the majors where they sold mosquito repellent at the concession stand. On their first trip into Houston, the Mets stayed at a motel that turned out to be a staging area for call girls. Other hotels wouldn't take them at first because of their Negro players. Once in the new Astrodome, the showers wouldn't work, and Casey Stengel complained bitterly, "They beat you and you can't even bathe." Ed Kranepool charged, not wholly in jest, that the Astro management manipulated the air conditioning in the Dome, making it blow out when the home team was at bat and in against the visitors. Rod Kanehl summed up the Mets' feeling about their fellow expansion city once and for all: "Houston, my ass!"

However, Koosman won on the next-to-last day of the season and, even though Seaver lost his final start the Mets finished ninth, a full game ahead of Houston.

Hodges was not around to buy champagne for this ninth-place finish as Westrum had done two years earlier. The season had been a bitter and frustrating one as he sought to take command of his new ball club and mold it to his image. (Cowboy hats had to be banned, he felt, after they had suddenly sprouted on several heads during one trip, and so did hippie love beads after two players, Don Cardwell and Ron Swoboda, who was wearing them, almost got into a fight.) As the Mets fought the specter of last place, Hodges grew more and more tense, his cigarette consumption rising from two to three packs a day.

The Mets were now on their last road trip, and Hodges was feeling poorly. He was experiencing strange chest pains. On September 24, Gil and his coaches left early as usual for a night game in the Atlanta ball park and the pains resumed. This time they were worse, "like a toothache," he later revealed. By the second inning, he had to leave the bench, and he put Walker in charge of the team. The Braves' physician suggested that Hodges rest easy and said he'd see him later if he didn't feel better. But Gus Mauch, trainer of the Mets, had been through a serious heart attack himself. He didn't like the sound of Hodges' symptoms. "Come on, I'm taking you to the hospital right now," he ordered. There, it was determined that Gil Hodges, only forty-four and still "strong enough to squeeze your ear-brows off," was suffering a heart attack.

Less than a month later, Gil was allowed to leave the hospital. Doctors said that if he followed their instructions there was no reason why he couldn't safely resume his managerial career. Although the Mets had set a club record of seventy-three victories in Hodges' first year, a lot of people wondered, "Why would he want to?" These were the same people who never really understood why Casey Stengel came back.

13

100-to-1

Dawn comes slowly in Saint Petersburg, Florida, heralded, at least at the Mets' Colonial Inn spring headquarters, by the croaking of sea gulls and the bleating of hungry seals in the aquarium next door. Gil Hodges, manager of the Mets, was awake. He dressed quickly and met coach Joe Pignatano, and together they crossed deserted Gulf Boulevard and strode off toward downtown. Gil Hodges, like his players, was getting in shape. His heart was making a comeback after a bad year. He and the faithful Piggy would walk a couple of miles and then the other coaches would pick them up and they'd all drive the rest of the way to Huggins-Stengel Field.

It was a spring training like most other spring trainings for the Mets. A lot of hope, not much talent beyond the pitching staff, and the usual wasted opportunities.

All through the winter the Mets had known that Richie Allen of the Phillies and Joe Torre of the Braves were available for trade. Allen, a notorious disciplinary problem, would have been available only for one of the Mets' top pitchers, Koosman or Seaver. John Murphy responded firmly in the negative, and few argued his decision. Torre, though, was another matter. A Brooklyn boy and a proven slugger, he was also capable of catching or playing first base with skill.

Torre was available at a comparative bargain price because he was coming off a bad year and a contract dispute. And he had become even more *non grata* with the Braves because of his strong role with the Major League Baseball Players Association, which had boycotted the early weeks of spring training because of a contract dispute with the owners.

The twenty-four major-league teams took varied approaches to the boycott. Some, like the Cardinals, put no pressure on their players to break the strike, fearing that scars from a bitter labor dispute would carry over to mar their happy-family formula. The Mets took a middle course. Fringe players were encouraged to sign and get a jump in competition for jobs. Some did, but most stayed away from Huggins-Stengel Field. Ed Kranepool remained in New York, where, as the Mets' player-rep, he was active in negotiations. Others, a group of about half a dozen, conducted their own informal training camp in the yard of Tom Seaver's rented house. Seaver, Bud Harrelson, Jerry Koosman, and the others worked out together regularly, and some of the team's close-knit feeling could be traced to these sessions.

The Atlanta Braves, however, struggled bitterly to break the strike and doubled their efforts to unload the outspoken Torre. A multiplayer deal was presented to the Mets. But when Murphy saw the name of Amos Otis on the list, he balked. Amos Otis, a rookie who had appeared in only nineteen big-league games back in 1967, was an "untouchable." The Mets planned to try him at third base this spring, but Murphy had another reason for wanting to keep strings on the young man whom several sportswriters had dubbed "Omis Atis." Tommie Agee had been such a flop the year before, Murphy thought Otis might be needed to take over in center field.

The deal was nixed at the last minute, and Paul Richards, general manager of the Braves, who had put together what he thought was an attractive package, was furious. "If they've got so many untouchables, how come they don't win any pennants?" he asked as he promptly traded Torre to the Cardinals.

As the Mets broke camp and headed north, Hodges made his annual prediction. "We will win a minimum of eighty-five games," he promised.

Eighty-five victories would put the Mets comfortably over .500, a plateau they had never before even approached. Nobody knew where this would put them in the standings, but the Mets had one consolation. They couldn't finish tenth again . . . or ninth . . . or even eighth. The majors had expanded anew, and each league was split into two six-team divisions. The Mets couldn't finish worse than sixth, and with one expansion team in each division, they ought to be no lower than fifth.

In Las Vegas, professional oddsmakers pegged the Mets' chances of winning the pennant at a feeble 100-to-1. Mrs. Charles Shipman Payson, owner of the Mets, confidently made plans to visit her children in Europe at the end of September, annually the most hopeless of times for her ball club. In New York, Dan Reilly, manager of the Mets' speakers' bureau, told his fiancée, Gloria Westerweller of Queens, to go ahead with their wedding plans for October 11. Nobody would want any Met speakers on the first day of a World Series. A promotion scheme was being hatched with the Borden's Company to provide cut-rate tickets for kids. Included in the program were sets of back-to-back games with the Cubs, July 8 and 9 and September 8 and 9, always dead spots in the schedule. And the football Jets, who shared Shea Stadium, made plans to stage their home opener against Boston on October 5.*

None of these plans seemed in jeopardy as the Mets opened their season at home on April 8. Tom Seaver was their pitcher, Shea Stadium was decked in bunting, and Montreal, one of the new expansion teams, was the opposition. The Mets, who had worried all along about their hitting, scored ten runs. The Expos, unimpressed by Seaver's reputation, scored eleven. The Amazin's' record remained intact. They are the only established team in baseball that has never won an opening game.

They got even the next day, however, and then won again when Tommie Agee became the first man ever to hit a home run into the upper deck at Shea Stadium. "That ball was hit 599 feet. Only God can hit 'em 600 feet," crowed Cleon Jones, Agee's pal and roomie. "The furthest ball ever hit at Shea," added Ron Swoboda.

But Agee was almost subdued over his home run. He looked down the hall toward Hodges' office. There was the man who had kept faith in him all through his self-described "ridiculous" first year as a Met. Don Bosch, the man who had preceded Agee as a

---

* Only the football team showed any foresight. The Jets made sure their early home opponents were teams they also would play on the road. When the Mets pre-empted the stadium, the dates were simply reversed. Mrs. Payson, too superstitious to change her plans, went ahead with her trip and was in Europe when the Mets surged to the pennant. Dan Reilly gave his bride precedence and got married on schedule. And while many got in, thousands of kids, clutching Borden's tickets, were shut out of those two big series with the Cubs.

center-field flop, was playing center field for the expansion Expos. Agee had reason to be grateful for a second chance and he knew it.

The Mets, though, showed few signs of being anything but their old lovable, inept selves. After his mammoth homer, Agee hit only one single in his next seventeen at-bats. Jerry Koosman hurt a shoulder and was out for almost a month. Jim McAndrew got a blister and was out for almost a month. Nolan Ryan pulled a groin muscle and went on the disabled list. And Gary Gentry, the rookie pitcher labeled as this year's Seaver, was giving up a lot of home runs.

Looking for some punch, Hodges struggled over his lineup cards each day. He knew the pitching would come around and that hitting was something you either had or didn't have. What galled this quiet leader were all the other mistakes the Mets were making to beat themselves. The Cubs were running off in the National League's Eastern Division. The heavily favored defending-champion Cardinals were a sleeping giant laying off the pace. The Mets were just sleeping in fifth place. Same old Mets.

A 6-5 loss to Atlanta on May 15 finally got the best of Hodges. It was the team's eighth one-run loss in less than six weeks of the new season, and one-run games separate winners from losers. For the first time since he took over as Met manager, Hodges locked the clubhouse door. There was no being "chewed out by a computer" this time.

"Heatedly exasperated," was one player's description of Hodges' tirade. "Lackadaisical . . . complacent . . . mental mistakes . . . recurrences"—these were some of the charges Hodges leveled at his young players, who sat stunned and silent in front of their lockers. No players were mentioned by name during Hodges' explosion, but specific incidents were. Every player knew when his turn came up. Hodges normally kept things to himself, and that's what helped make his lecture more effective.

"We could be a first-division club but we can't afford these mistakes," he told his players, and six days later Tom Seaver shut out the Braves and the Mets were at .500 at the latest date in their history. "It doesn't mean a thing," Tom Seaver snapped. He and his teammates refused to measure themselves against the futility of the past.

A week later, Hodges suddenly realized that he was hitting a lot of grounders in pre-game infield practice. That was good, not so much as a sign that his health was restored, but that the Mets were winning. It had become a tradition with Gil and his close-knit coaching staff that they would take turns during the formal pre-game infield drill. However, if the Mets won, the same man would continue with that chore until they lost.

On May 28, the Mets started an eleven-game winning streak. They swept the Giants and they swept the Dodgers, and when they played them again a week later, they swept them again. The Giants and the Dodgers. These young Mets were exorcizing past ghosts. No longer was this team merely a substitute for those departed heroes of yesteryear. The late Charlie Dressen had once gained a measure of fame by declaring, prematurely as well as ungrammatically, "The Giants is dead." With this double sweep, the Mets were announcing, "The Giants and Dodgers is dead. . . . Long live the Mets!"

Even Hodges, normally so disinclined to see omens, had to admit those sweeps "gave us confidence."

As the season headed into June, it became apparent that Hodges' lecture had awakened the Mets, and now their pitching was sound. Seaver was Seaver, as always. Koosman was showing anew that no pitcher in baseball is tougher with a lead in the late innings. And Gentry was overcoming those early lapses. The backup starters were Jim McAndrew, veteran Don Cardwell, and Nolan Ryan. Ron Taylor and Cal Koonce returned as the right-handed side of the bullpen. And two newcomers, Tug McGraw and Jack DiLauro, were there to get out the lefties. McGraw had been with the Mets before. He was one of Casey Stengel's Youth of America in 1965. But in 1968 he hadn't pitched an inning in the majors. Immaturity was dooming this handsome, likable lad to a life sentence in the minors. But he grew up in 1969. DiLauro also had been a career minor-leaguer. "If you need a guy to get that one left-hander out, he's your man," the scouts told Hodges, and during the season DiLauro was called up to do just that.

Putting them all together, it was a classic pitching staff, strong in all categories. Rotund Rube Walker was the housemother. When other pitching staffs collapsed from overwork in September, Met arms were still alive. That was Walker's achievement.

Still, despite Cleon Jones' fine start and Tommie Agee's resurgence, the Mets continued to be short of crunch. With the trading deadline approaching, Johnny Murphy continued to work on a deal.

On June 15, the final day of free trading, he got it: Donn Clendenon from Montreal for infielder Kevin Collins and three minor-league pitchers, Steve Renko, Jay Carden, and Dave Colon. Clendenon, a month short of his thirty-fourth birthday, had been one of those major-leaguers who seemed to just miss stardom. When he came up to the Pirates, it appeared the lanky first-baseman could do everything—hit with power, run with rare speed for a big man, and field his position with facility. He could also strike out a lot, especially against right-handed pitching. "I always had the feeling they wanted me to be another Dick Stuart," Clendenon said of his days with the Pirates. So he swung for the fences every time up, and most of the time he came up empty. After eight years with the Pirates, he was exposed on the expansion list, and Montreal made him its sixth pick. The Expos didn't keep him, however, and in late February traded Clendenon and outfielder Jesus Alou to Houston for Rusty Staub.

Staub was delighted with the deal, moved to Montreal, and began hawking tickets for his new club. Alou reported, too, when spring training began, but Clendenon went home to Atlanta and announced his retirement. A lawyer on top of his other talents (he plays the trumpet), Clendenon held an executive position with the Scripto pen company and also owned a supper club in Atlanta. The Astro management howled at Clendenon's defection. They wanted the deal canceled. Baseball Commissioner Bowie Kuhn then stepped in. Clendenon was retired, he was coming back, it was off, it was on, it was a mess. Finally Kuhn arranged for Montreal to send Houston another player, with Clendenon returning to the Expos under a new two-year contract.

Undergoing only five days of "spring training," Clendenon by June 15 had hit only four home runs in thirty-eight games for a .240 average. Welcoming the trade to New York, he said enthusiastically, "I'm ready to be a Met the rest of my life."

With Clendenon's arrival, Hodges had his lineup virtually set, but it was not a set lineup. Following the Stengel principle, Hodges played with a twenty-five-man squad, not just eight regulars. Did Clendenon have trouble with right-handed pitching? He and Ed Kranepool, a lefty batter, would share first base. Both would play, both would contribute and, more important, both would know they were contributing.

The only full-time regulars were Bud Harrelson, a switch-hitter,

Al Weis

Jerry Grote

Art Shamsky

at short; Jerry Grote behind the plate; Tommie Agee in center field, and Cleon Jones in left.

Ken Boswell played most of the games at second base because most pitchers are right-handed and Boswell bats left. Al Weis and Bobby Pfeil also played second against lefties, and Weis, an outstanding fielder, also spelled Harrelson at short. Wayne Garrett played third against righties, Ed Charles took over against lefties. Left-handed hitting Art Shamsky and righty Ron Swoboda shared right field. When defense was of the essence, Rod Gaspar played right.

Everybody was a player and everybody cared. Nobody got fat and out of shape. Because the Mets were so young, many of their players had to leave for two-week and weekend tours of military duty. When this happened, the substitute was ready to play because he hadn't been sitting on the bench all summer. Ed Charles, the elder statesman and gentle poet laureate, put it best when the Mets started winning. "A lot of the credit goes to Number 14," he said, nodding toward Hodges and referring to the way the manager had manipulated and inspired his squad.

The Mets had swept aside the past in that double sweep over the Giants and the Dodgers in June. They began work on the future in July. In past years, a "crucial" series for the Mets had involved games with Houston that always determined the New Yorkers would be finishing last again. Now, the Mets had their eyes looking forward, not back. The Cubs were coming to town for three games, and then, four days later, the Mets would go to Chicago for three more. If they could win four of those next six games with Chicago, the Mets would be contenders for real. The right-hand column of the league standings showed that New York was five games behind Chicago going into this head-to-head series. But the second column from the left was more significant. That was what baseball writers refer to mockingly as the "all-important" loss column. The Mets had played fewer games than the Cubs at this stage. They were only two games down in the loss column. That was the real measure of the distance between these two teams.

More than 55,000 fans, many of them Borden's kids, jammed Shea Stadium for the series opener July 8. Jerry Koosman opened for the Mets and was opposed by Chicago's ace, Ferguson Jenkins, a Canadian right-hander who attacks his job with such verve that he runs out to the mound at the start of each inning.

Ed Kranepool and Ernie Banks traded early home runs, but the Cubs went into the ninth inning with a 3-1 lead. Kranepool's homer had been the Mets' only hit, and the Cubs' third run had come on a homer by Jim Hickman. Yes, Jim Hickman, the original Met. "Funny, after all those years with the Mets I'm finally in a position to make some money, and who's trying to take it away from me but the Mets," he mused that afternoon before confiding quietly, "You know, we haven't been playing very good ball the last couple of weeks. I hope it doesn't start catching up with us."

But in the last of the ninth, Hickman's words took on the ring of ominous prophecy for Chicago. Ken Boswell and Donn Clendenon opened with pinch-hit doubles, both of which were misplayed by rookie center-fielder Don Young. Those hits put men on second and third, and Cleon Jones singled them both home for the tie. A walk and an out later, Ed Kranepool singled to left field, and Cleon scampered home with the winning run. The Mets won, 4-3, and the Cubs' lead was down to four games—only one in the lost column.

Fans started lining up hours before the gates even opened for the next night's game, hoping for a precious seat or even a place to stand or squat. As the crowd of 59,083 gathered (the biggest ever in Shea history, although, because of the Borden's deal, only 50,709 were registered as paid), word began to spread about signs of Cub panic after the previous day's loss. Leo Durocher, the Cubs' cocky and abrasive manager, had publicly stated that Young should have caught both fly balls in his direction. And Ron Santo, the team captain and third-baseman, had called Young "a disgrace to

After one season, Tommie Agee could do it all.

the game" for allegedly brooding over his batting slump when he should have been concentrating on fly balls.

Santo had been enraging opposing players by his habit of leaping in the air and kicking his heels after each Cub victory. "A bush trick," they scowled. Now he was enraging his own players. Before the game he apologized privately to Young, then to his teammates in the clubhouse, and, finally, in public to Chicago newsmen. But the damage had been done. While Santo was completing his apologies, Tom Seaver was beginning to warm up for the Mets. Funny, but his shoulder felt a little tight. "Oh, well, it will work itself out," he thought.

The Cubs presented their usual lineup against Seaver, except instead of Young in center field, Durocher went with another rookie, Jimmy Qualls. However, Durocher insisted that this was because right-hander Seaver was starting for the Mets instead of lefty Koosman. Qualls, unlike Young, was a left-handed hitter. He had just come up from the minors, and this was only his eighteenth major-league game. Few of the Mets knew how to pitch to him or where to play him. "He hits the ball all over and generally makes contact," one player volunteered, remembering half a season or so in some forgotten bush league a couple of years back.

A pennant race, a huge crowd, a balmy summer night, and two fine pitchers, Seaver against Ken Holtzman. "It was a night for great things," one reporter said to himself as he idly framed a preliminary lead in his mind. The Mets got a run, then a few more. Holtzman was replaced by Ted Abernathy. The Mets were rolling.

Meanwhile, Seaver forgot about the stiffness in his shoulder. Adrenalin, pulsating and racing through the system, is a great painkiller. He struck out five of the first six Cubs he faced, and in the dugout pitching coach Rube Walker turned to Hodges and said, "He's got enough stuff to pitch a no-hitter."

Seaver continued in command, extending his dominance with every pitch. The Cubs saw him getting stronger and were helpless. No-hitter? Tom Seaver was pitching a perfect game. Three in a row, three in a row, three in a row. Not even a really tough chance for his fielders. And with every pitch, the huge crowd, caught in the mounting hysteria, joined in cheering Tom Seaver on, nearly 60,000 people fused in one heroic figure driving for perfection.

The unbroken cheers of encouragement grew louder as Seaver headed into the ninth inning. Randy Hundley, the catcher, was leading off for the Cubs, then Qualls, then a pinch-hitter for the pitcher.

The last perfect game at Shea had been Father's Day in 1964. Jim Bunning, father of seven (at the time), had done it to the Mets for the Phillies. His wife and one of his children were in the stands for that game. Seaver was childless, but his pretty wife Nancy, and his father, visiting from California, were watching in the packed stadium. The Mets had been no-hit a lot of times. They'd never had one of their own.

Randy Hundley, a tough catcher who once got over $100,000 to sign, led off and squared away to bunt on the first pitch. That's the gut-pro way to break up a no-hitter, and the crowd jeered even as Seaver fielded the ball and threw him out. Then came Qualls. Seaver was throwing mostly fast balls now, and Qualls would have trouble pulling the ball to right field. But in center, Agee was afraid to shade the rookie because he already had fulfilled the meager scouting report by hitting for outs to both sides of the diamond. So he played him straight away. Seaver took the sign, fast ball, and went into his motion. The ball sped in, a little higher than Seaver intended, and out over the plate. A pitch to hit and Qualls did. His line drive to left center fell between Agee and Cleon Jones. If Agee had moved over, maybe he could have got to it, but, then, maybe Qualls would have hit in the other direction. Tom Seaver stood rooted on the mound staring out to where the ball had dropped. He was completely drained, the adrenalin flowed out of his system as if somebody had pulled a plug. Jerry Grote went out to get Seaver's mind back on business, and the husky right-hander retired the next two batters to complete the 4-0, one-hit victory.

As Nancy Seaver cried in sharing her husband's disappointment, the Cubs' lead was trimmed to only three games.

The next afternoon, the Cubs salvaged the last game of the series, 6-2. "Were those the real Cubs we saw today?" somebody asked Durocher. "No, but those were the real Mets," he snarled in derision. "Wait till we get them in Wrigley Field," Santo warned.

After regaining their composure with four games against Montreal, the Mets went out to Chicago. The Cubs had been killing the opposition in their Wrigley Field den. A raucous gang of fans who had dubbed themselves the "Bleacher Bums" inhabited the left-field bleacher section. Dick Selma, the flaky former Met, was their cheerleader. They wore yellow construction helmets and they showered enemy left-fielders with debris and obscenities.

The Cubs won that first game, 1-0, as Santo did his little ballet leap of triumph, but then the Mets came back as they had been doing all season. Dick Selma was the pitcher, and Al Weis, little Al Weis, Al Weis, who had hit only four home runs in six previous major-league seasons, hit a three-run homer as the Mets scored a 5-4 victory. And the next day he hit another one and so did Tommie Agee and the Mets knocked out Ferguson Jenkins after one inning and Ron Santo did no dance of joy. But Tom Seaver did. "Wait till we get them back in Chicago," he mimicked after the 9-5 victory, and Al Weis pleaded humbly, "Now don't try to make me out a home-run hitter. In fact, I'm not even a hitter."

But when a team is challenging for a pennant, it needs Al Weis and others of his ilk to emerge as heroes. Just before the All-Star break, the Mets went into the tenth inning of the second game of a doubleheader in Montreal all even, 3-3. Bobby Pfeil, the kid who had spent eight years in the bushes, a throw-in on a minor-league deal, squeezed home the winning run. Bobby Pfeil had signed his first pro contract in 1962, the year the Mets were born. They were both arriving at the same time.

Incredible

The Mets were in trouble. They may have been amazing to the rest of the world, but to the Houston Astros, née Colt .45s, they were still the runt of the 1962 National League expansion litter. On July 30, in Shea Stadium, the Astros beat the Mets, 16-3 and 11-5. They scored 11 runs in the ninth inning of the first game and 10 runs in the third inning of the second game.

During the second-game outburst, Johnny Edwards hit a double to the left-field corner on which Cleon Jones gave tentative chase and then a lob throw to the infield. Time was called as Hodges moved with deliberate speed out of the dugout. But he hadn't come on the field to remove a pitcher. He walked right past the mound and to left field. "Are you hurt?" he asked Jones sarcastically. "You must be hurt," he answered himself, and he turned on his heel and walked back to the dugout with the shocked and humiliated Cleon Jones trailing several paces behind.

At the time, the twenty-seven-year-old outfielder was batting .350 and leading the National League. Once shy and introverted, Cleon continued to blossom as a personality and a player. Although much was made, and rightly so, of the Pfeils and Garretts who were winning games for the Mets in their merry chase, those sporadic contributions would have been valueless without day-in-and-day-out star play by such as Cleon Jones, who ended up batting .340, third-best in the league, and by Agee, who led the team with twenty-six home runs.

Although Hodges at first tried to claim that Jones was indeed hurt, nobody worked very hard at concealing the true significance of Cleon's public removal from the game. Hodges was getting tough. The Mets were sagging and the manager, to show that his wrath played no favorites, had picked the team's leading hitter for discipline. "It looked like what you guys thought it was," Jones said glumly to reporters, admitting he had been "embarrassed" by Hodges' unprecedented public display. (Later Jones would say, "I was very belittled. If I didn't respect what the man was trying to do, I could very easily hate his guts, but I don't.")

The next day, Hodges benched second-baseman Ken Boswell as the Astros won, 2-0, to complete the sweep and make it six in a row against the Mets. "Is he hurt, too?" somebody asked. "His play is hurting," the manager snapped.

And Ron Swoboda, at this point an almost forgotten Met—"I'm the third-string pinch-runner," he complained—decided to speak up. "This whole bunch needs dedication," he charged. "We tra-la-lahed through the doubleheader with an air of gaiety."

But most of the Mets simply wondered, Who the hell is he to say anything? and the slide continued. On August 13, the Mets finished blowing another series to Houston, this time three straight in the Astrodome. They were in third place, nine and a half games behind the division-leading Cubs.

However, before the week was out, the Mets had swept consecutive doubleheaders from San Diego. For a change it was their turn to get well against an expansion team, and the tonic worked. Including the four against the Padres, the Mets won twelve of their next thirteen and, just as suddenly, the Cubs were stumbling. With a rush, these two teams careened toward each other, the Mets gathering drive and momentum and belief in themselves as they surged upward, the Cubs, wracked with self-doubt and torn by the sulks and rages and absences of their abrasive manager, Leo Durocher, plummeting on a downhill toboggan. On September 8, at Shea Stadium, they collided.

The Cubs still had the lead, but they were pressing—and they showed it in the very first inning. Jerry Koosman had started for the Mets and retired the Cubs without incident in the top half. Then Bill Hands, a New Jersey lad who had been quite successful against the Mets in the past, went to the mound for Chicago. Tommie Agee was the first Met batter, and Hands' first pitch went flying in the general direction of his batting helmet. It was the

The day after they routed the Mets in a doubleheader,
the Astros won again at Shea Stadium, 2—0.
Here Denis Menke scores for Houston
as his hard slide forces Jerry Grote to drop the ball.

classic Durocher ploy, the intimidator; what Branch Rickey, who,
mercy sakes, would never recommend throwing at a batter, used
to call the "purpose pitch." Its purpose was to scare hell out of
you. Maybe the old Mets would have been scared, but now they
saw this dust-off pitch as a symbol of Cub concern and weakness.
Agee had gone sprawling into the dirt to avoid being hit, and even
before he finished dusting himself off, Jerry Koosman knew what
he had to do.

The Cubs' leadoff batter in the second inning was Ron Santo, the
heel-kicker. Santo should have had a notion. Koosman's first pitch
came veering inside, toward his rib cage, and as Santo pulled
away, the ball hit him on the wrist. ("You gonna hit a guy, you

don't throw at his head, you throw in here," Casey Stengel used to advise, motioning toward the chest. "If you're lucky, you also get a piece of the bat and it's only a foul ball.")

Later Santo had to leave the game, and Koosman finally conceded, "Sure I did it on purpose. You've got to protect your teammates." Durocher's strategy not only had failed to intimidate the Mets but also cost him his team captain and one of his leading hitters in a big game. It became a double failure when Agee hit a two-run homer his next time at bat. And after the Cubs had tied in the sixth, Agee doubled and scored the winning run on a close play at the plate. Koosman, decked himself by a retaliatory pitch later in the game, struck out thirteen in the 3-2 victory, and the next night Seaver pitched a five-hitter as the Mets won, 7-1, for a sweep of the two-game set.

The Cubs dragged out of town with only half a game of their nine-and-a-half-game lead remaining, muttering about Met pitchers, "Who do they think they are? They think they own the league." The Mets had a one-game edge in the loss column, and their fans chorused derisively as Seaver was completing his victory, "Goodbye, Leo; Goodbye, Leo . . ." A sea of white handkerchiefs fluttered at the Cub dugout.

The Mets were enjoying their victory after the game, sipping beer in various stages of undress. (It's a mark of a happy, winning team when players like to hang around the clubhouse after a game.) But suddenly they were thrown into a state of panic. Was Leo Durocher coming in to lick them all himself? Not hardly.

"Mrs. Payson is coming, Mrs. Payson is coming," Nick Torman, the equipment manager, trumpeted. "Get your pants on!" Yes, indeed, it was Mrs. Payson, overcome with joy, on her way to congratulate her boys. First she and her entourage, led by M. Donald Grant, went into Hodges' office. "Oh, Gil, you've made me so happy," she gushed. "I'm so thrilled I can hardly stand. I have to give you a kiss."

And she did.

"I'll be here tomorrow when you go into first place," she promised, and then she marched into the clubhouse proper to greet the players. Not a bare leg was in sight. "If you don't get your pants on, you'll be playing for Tidewater [the Mets' top farm team] next year," Ed Charles had warned, and all the basic dressing was

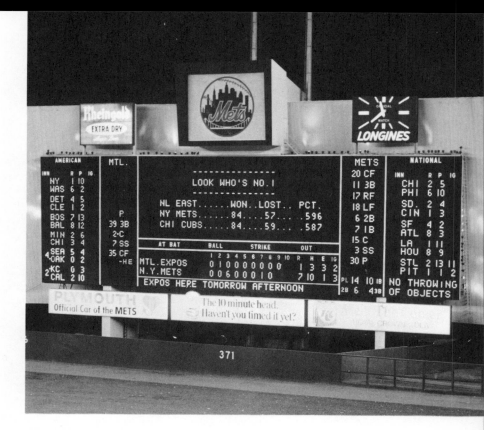

The scoreboard tells it all.

completed in time. She saluted the old players and was introduced to the new boys. "I'll be here tomorrow," she repeated. "Good luck."

The next day, the Cubs obliged by losing to Philadelphia, 6-2, but the Mets by now almost resented getting help to move into first place. The mystique of momentum was theirs. That night they downed the Expos, 3-2, in the first game of a doubleheader on Ken Boswell's twelfth-inning single to take over first place. And then they won the second game, too. "Look Who's No. 1," the scoreboard bragged as the standings flashed below.

In the stands, Mrs. Payson was weeping. After all these years, first place!

Some of the Mets had prepared for this moment. That afternoon, Bud Harrelson, Ron Swoboda, Tug McGraw, and Ed Kranepool had visited a Brooklyn winery and each had been given several

Mrs. Payson is overjoyed as she visits the clubhouse to congratulate
Gil Hodges and his players on attaining first place.

bottles of champagne. "If we get a big lead in the second game,
put it on ice," Harrelson told Nick Torman. And when the Mets
scored six runs in the third inning to start the 7-1 rout, Torman
came out to the bench and gave Harrelson an inquiring look.
"Put it on," Bud said.

There wasn't enough champagne for showers and shampoos, but
the taste was good. "You don't go into first place every day,"
Harrelson growled.

More than three weeks still remained in the season, but the Mets
were starting their countdown to glory.

On September 11, Gary Gentry shut out the Expos with a six-
hitter. The next day the Mets swept the Pirates in a doubleheader
by identical 1-0 scores as Jerry Koosman and Don Cardwell, the
pitchers, drove in the only runs. On the 13th, the Mets ran their
winning streak to ten in a row by beating the Pirates, 5-2, on Ron

Swoboda's grand-slam home run. Ron Swoboda, who earlier in the year had set a record for consecutive strikeouts, was now a hero. It seemed only right. Two nights later Steve Carlton of the Cardinals set a major-league record by striking out nineteen Mets. He got the record, but not the victory. Swoboda hit a pair of two-run homers, and the Mets won again, 4-3. It was incredible.

Even when the Mets lost, it was something. On September 20, Bob Moose of the Pirates stopped them with a no-hitter. But the next night Koosman and Cardwell beat Pittsburgh in another doubleheader to start a nine-game winning streak that ran to the final game of the season.

Three days after Moose's no-hitter, the Mets' countdown reached its final numbers. The Cardinals were in town and Bob Gibson, one of the great Met-killers, was their pitcher. Jim McAndrew, the psychologist, went for the home team as over 32,000 sat in noisy attendance. Eleven innings it took, and in the end the Mets prevailed again, 3-2. The hero? Note him closely. Ron Swoboda made a great catch and scored the winning run and then sat exultantly on home plate giving a victory sign. Gibson had humiliated Swoboda many times, too.

In the clubhouse, Gil Hodges opened a telegram: "Happy to see you're No. 1. Hope your team does as well as your heart. Linton H. Bishop, Jr., M.D." Dr. Bishop was Hodges' doctor in Atlanta. The Mets had clinched at least a tie for their division title on the first anniversary of Gil's heart attack.

More than 54,000 fans, tense and explosive, jammed Shea Stadium the following night to share in history. It was the Cardinals again with Steve Carlton, the strikeout king, as starting pitcher. Many years ago, the bumbling Mets had delayed a St. Louis pennant clinching on the final weekend of the season. Maybe the Cards could give it back to them.

The Met pitching choice was Gary Gentry, the hard-eyed, sharp-featured rookie, already successful heir to the Koosman-Seaver tradition of first-year excellence. Gentry had won eleven games and lost twelve and had the confidence of a twenty-game winner. Lack of confidence was never Gary Gentry's problem. He had helped his junior college win a national championship in 1965 and he had led Arizona State to a national championship two years later with a 17-1 record. During these great years, he was drafted by the Orioles, the Astros, and the Giants, and he turned them all down. "Wants upwards of $70,000 to sign," stated one report, and who wanted to give that kind of money to a skinny 175-pounder even if he could throw BBs through brick walls? Baseball had instituted its free-agent draft for the express purpose of cutting down on bonus demands, and only the top first-round picks were able to command any kind of money to sign.

In June of 1967, the Mets took a crack at drafting Gentry. Maybe they'd get lucky. Scout Dee Fondy had been shadowing him for three years, winning his friendship. He and Joe McDonald, director of Met minor-league operations, followed Gentry to the College World Series in Omaha, but once there they ignored the boy off the field. As the days went by, Gentry became the star of the tournament, but he wondered what the matter was with his good friend Dee Fondy. The Mets had drafted him, but maybe they weren't interested any more? The ploy worked. When it came time to talk contract, Gentry agreed to sign for a realistic bonus of about $20,000. The Mets sent him right off to the fast Double AA Eastern League, and the next season he was jumped to Triple A and from there to the Mets. "Shows stamina and courage on the mound," read his early reports, and these were the attributes that had won him a chance to pitch the possible title-clincher.

Gentry's teammates made it easy for him. Bud Harrelson led off with a single and Tommie Agee walked. Cleon Jones had been out for two weeks with hand and rib injuries (real, not disciplinary), but he put himself back in the lineup for this game, wanting so much to be a part of what it all meant. Cleon struck out this time, but Donn Clendenon followed with a three-run homer over the center-field wall. Ron Swoboda walked and then Ed Charles, The Glider, in the self-admitted "twilight" of his career, drilled a home run over the wall in left and clapped his way around the bases "to show everybody how it felt." That was it. Clendenon later hit another home run, and Gentry pitched a four-hitter as the Mets won, 6-0.

The crowd poised almost like sprinters in the starting blocks as Gentry and the Mets moved into the ninth inning. With two on and one out, Joe Torre came to bat for St. Louis—Joe Torre, the star Johnny Murphy had failed to obtain in a deal with Atlanta that spring. Getting Torre would have meant a pennant for the Mets, they all said. Tonight he hit into a game-ending double play . . . that meant a pennant for the Mets.

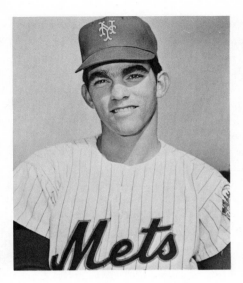

Rookie Gary Gentry pitched the clincher.

As Al Weis was turning over the double play and winging the ball to Clendenon at first, a tremendous surge of fans moved in a giant wave toward the playing field. Ushers and special police were helpless. Met players were engulfed as they raced off the field, losing their caps to the advancing horde. Down on the diamond the fans went, stripping sod, tearing up home plate, grabbing the bases in an orgy of happy destruction. One youth tried to scale the scoreboard and fell off, breaking his leg. Another posted a banner high atop the flagpole: "We've come a long way, baby."

And down in the clubhouse, during the pandemonium, a heavy, dark-browed cigar smoker with a twinkle in his eye remembered that the first Met banner of all time had been dedicated to him. Rod Kanehl, the mostest Met of them all, had come East from his home in Los Angeles just to be part of the clinching ceremony. "I had to be here," he said simply. And then he spotted another of the old losers, Craig Anderson. Now business manager of athletics at Lehigh University, Anderson had lost nineteen games in a row over three seasons for the Mets. His streak was still open, he could add to it anytime he cared to make a comeback, but it wasn't their time any more. "Who was that?" asked Tommie Agee after being introduced to Rod Kanehl.

"How far they gonna go? Why, they're amazing. Why, I'll tell you they're gonna go all the way to Baltimore," Casey Stengel exploded over the phone from Glendale, California.

In the clubhouse, the first of the wild champagne parties was under way. Coaches, Hodges, sportswriters, all were dragged under the showers. Other bystanders were drenched with champagne. "Hey, this stuff burns your eyes," Tug McGraw exclaimed at the thrill of discovery.

Mrs. Payson got word her team had clinched the division title while she was ill with bronchitis in London. And out in California, the Giants and the San Diego Padres were playing a baseball game. Roger Craig was San Diego's pitching coach and Chris Cannizzaro, Casey's old "Canzonari," was one of the catchers. The next night Craig was sending a young man out to pitch what might be his twentieth losing game. What Craig had suffered in losing twenty for the Mets would help him in guiding the rookie. "It's amazing," he said of the Mets' success, and that's what Cannizzaro, and the whole world, said: "Amazing."

On the other side of the field, sad-eyed and red-faced, as always, Wes Westrum sat in the uniform of a Giant coach and said, "Isn't it wonderful? Didn't I tell you they were going to be good soon? I knew all about those great arms when I left." And Ron Hunt, the Mets' first real All-Star, finished batting practice with the Giants and grumped in character, "Yeah, it's really amazing and great for baseball. I'm glad for the fans and for Mrs. Payson. They're the greatest and they deserve it. But as for M. Donald Grant, he can kiss my foot."

And back in New York, M. Donald Grant was pronouncing, "Our players have finally caught up with our fans."

And out on the field, the fans, it developed, had pulled a Throneberry. While stealing everything that wasn't riveted down, they had missed first base.

"The team has changed but the fans haven't," sportswriter Dick Young declared. But at least the fans hadn't missed second base, too, like old Marvelous. Maybe things were getting better.

15

They Could End a War

"What I want," Ed Kranepool had been saying, "is to come into Wrigley Field for those last two games of the season with a three-game lead and to be able to tell Ernie Banks, 'What a great day for baseball, eh, Ernie?' "

Well, it almost happened that way. Only the Mets came into Wrigley Field for the last two games of the season with an eight-game lead and the division championship not only in the bank but already drawing interest. Ernie Banks, the greatest of the Cubs, exclaimed through his disappointment, "What a great day for baseball!" as he always does, while Ed Kranepool kept his mouth shut because you don't rub it in with a guy like Ernie Banks.

The Mets won the first game of that anticlimactic final set, 6-5, in twelve innings. The losing pitcher was Dick Selma, and Jim Hickman was in the outfield, and some of the old Met writers recalled Casey Stengel's prophecy that "this here team won't win anything until we spread enough of our players around the league and make the other teams horseshit, too." By beating the Cubs, the Mets ran their winning streak to nine straight with their hundredth victory and, of the four divisional winners in the two major leagues, only the Orioles won more.

The next day, the Cubs took the final game of the season, 5-3, as one of the Bleacher Bums threw a smoke bomb on the field and Ernie Banks, gentleman, vowed he would attend the World Series "to see the Mets take it all."

But first, as they say in television, a word from the Braves. For all the excitement in Shea, the Mets had clinched only half a pennant, the National League's Eastern Division. They had to take on the champions of the West, Atlanta. Even though they had a better record, and had beaten the Braves eight of the twelve times they'd met, the Mets, as usual, were underdogs at 13-to-10 odds in the best-of-five series. The Mets had pitching, but the Braves had power —and the home field for the first two games.

It was overcast in Atlanta on Saturday afternoon, October 4, and the game was starting at the unusual hour of 4:00 p.m. as a sop to television. Phil Niekro, the Braves' knuckleballing twenty-three-game winner who had lost three decisions to the Mets during the season, was starting for the home team. Tom Seaver, who had won twenty-five, was the choice, as expected, for New York. Luman Harris, manager of the Braves, was reminded that but for a technicality Seaver would have been wearing an Atlanta uniform for this inaugural playoff. "Would he have been your opening pitcher today?" somebody asked Harris.

"I don't really know," the manager drawled diplomatically, "but I do know who my first two pitchers would have been."

Both choices, as the game developed, were less than perfect. Niekro was struggling from the beginning and so was Seaver. Maybe it was Seaver's week-long layoff after the title-clinching, maybe it was the unusual starting time. His control was off, he was missing his spots, and the Braves were hitting him.

But the Mets were hitting the Braves, too, which was not expected. A couple of base hits, a walk, a passed ball, and the Mets had a 2-0 lead in the second inning. However, Rico Carty doubled and scored in the Braves' turn, and then the home team added two more in the third for a 3-2 lead. The Mets went back in front with two in the fourth, but once again Seaver was unable to hold his lead. Tony Gonzalez slugged a homer in the fifth, and Henry Aaron hit one in the seventh to put the Braves back on top, 5-4.

Two innings to go and Seaver struggling. The Mets were like fancy-Dan boxers forced into a slugging match. Remember Billy Conn? He once tried to slug it out with Joe Louis and blew the heavyweight championship by getting knocked out when he only had to coast the final rounds. Were the Braves getting ready to kayo the Mets?

Wayne Garrett, freckle-faced Wayne Garrett, refugee from the Braves' farm system, was leading off the eighth for the Mets. His

Phil Niekro delivers the first pitch of the playoff to Tommie Agee.

average was an uninspiring .218, but the Mets' left-handed third-baseman slashed a double past Clete Boyer at third. It was the kind of hit that Boyer, one of baseball's finest fielders, might have come up with on many days. But this was not one of those days. Cleon Jones, a legitimate threat, then followed with a pop-fly single to left, and the score was tied. Art Shamsky added a single to right, his third hit, and the Mets had the winning run, represented by Jones, in scoring position at second.

With none out, the book called for a sacrifice, and Ken Boswell drew the sign for a bunt. But he missed the ball, and the Braves had Cleon Jones hung up off second base. On a play like this, the fielder with the ball, in this case rookie catcher Bob Didier, must run directly at the base runner and force him to commit himself before making a throw. If he must throw, he throws to the base in front of the runner to keep him from advancing. Up in Boston, Weeb Ewbank, coach of New York's football Jets, was watching the game on television. "You learn to make that play in high school," he snorted as the flustered Didier pegged blindly to second base behind Jones, who simply lit off for third.

With the winning run at third and none out, the Braves had to pull their infield in to try for an out at the plate. It's a calculated risk. It was a Casey Stengel axiom that "with the infield in, you oughta hit .400." It always annoyed him that in this situation batters wouldn't play "butcher boy." By hitting down on the ball—like a butcher chopping meat—they would assure a ground ball that, if it didn't go directly at a fielder, should make it through the infield.

Boswell, still at bat, did hit his ground ball, but right back at Niekro. It might have been a double play, but with Jones now on third, the pitcher had to check him there and was able to get only a force at second. Thus mental errors, like ripples from rocks thrown in a lake, compound themselves.

With men on first and third and one out, the Braves' infield could drop back a few steps to choose between a double play or a play at the plate on any ground ball. And Ed Kranepool obliged by hitting an easy grounder to Orlando Cepeda at first base. Cepeda had Jones dead at home, and Cleon even slowed down, hoping to force a rundown so the other runners could move up. But the baseball gods gripped Cepeda's arm with icicle fingers of indecision. Instead of firing home on instinct, he took careful aim and the ball skidded into the dirt a dozen feet in front of Didier and skipped by him for an error. Jones trotted home with the lead run. Shamsky only got to second on the play, but he and Kranepool moved up a base on Jerry Grote's infield out and Bud Harrelson was intentionally walked. The bases were loaded.

Seaver was due up now. A fine athlete, this chunky right-hander, and not a bad hitter, either. He led the pitching staff in hits and runs batted in. Even if he made out, he was the ace. He could get them in the last two innings and hold a one-run lead. He could, couldn't he? Couldn't he? Gil Hodges was not so sure. Seaver had been struggling all game. He had failed to protect several leads during the afternoon, and the bullpen was ready.

J. C. Martin, a spare catcher with a .209 average, got the call to hit for Seaver. With the bases loaded, Niekro could not take a chance on walking Martin, which not only would force in a run but also would bring up the dangerous Agee. His first pitch had to be a strike, and he could not risk starting off with his erratic knuckleball. That first pitch had to be a fast ball, and the Mets knew Niekro's fast ball was no more than ordinary. Joseph Clifton Martin was waiting for it and ready to swing. Waiting just right and not trying to kill the ball, Martin stroked Niekro's first pitch softly into center field. Shamsky scored, Kranepool scored, and as the ball got by Gonzalez for Atlanta's second error of the inning, Harrelson scored, too.

Through it all, Martin kept running, knowing that if the Braves tried to get him they would concede that third run, and they finally threw him out at third to end the inning. The Mets had scored five runs, in a "textbook" inning that included all the horrible examples by the Braves, for a 9-5 victory.

What's a laugher? A laugher is when your team gets eight runs in the first four innings and the other team doesn't get any and, by the fifth inning you lead, 9-1. That's a laugher, and that's what the Mets had with Jerry Koosman pitching in the second game of the National League playoffs. The laughs froze on their faces in the last of the fifth, however, when the Braves scored five runs to pull up to 9-6. With Atlanta's power, any Met lapses could be followed by a game-tying home run. The situation was suddenly grim, and in the seventh inning all the joy and happiness of the Mets' glorious season was almost erased in a stunning near-tragedy.

With one out, Tommie Agee drew a walk, stole second, and, with two down, was perched on third. Cleon Jones, his boyhood friend, was at bat. The count was two balls and a strike when Tommie Agee decided to try to steal home.

There's no sign on a play like this. The runner just hopes the hitter sees him coming and sometimes he'll yell, "Look out!" as he shifts into high gear. Cleon saw Agee coming out of the corner of his eye, but he didn't react. Cecil Upshaw was on the mound for the Braves, and he gave Cleon a pretty good pitch to hit. So he did, hooking a line drive just foul past the left-field pole. Cleon had swung with all his might and his backswing carried him around. As Agee was sliding into the plate, Cleon's bat came within inches of bashing his friend in the head.

Stunned and shocked, like survivors of a terrible automobile wreck, the two close friends walked slowly around home plate to regain their composure. They meant so much to each other, these former high school teammates and neighbors. Agee had helped draw Jones out of his immature shell of shyness, Cleon had helped nurse Tommie through a depressing winter after his dismal debut with the Mets. What made the near-miss even more traumatic, dozens of their friends and neighbors from nearby Mobile were in the stands. Their holiday almost had a tragic conclusion.

"If he had hit me, it might have been all over," Agee said later.

When they regained their cool, Jones asked his buddy, "What were you trying to do, cheat me out of a run batted in?" And Agee trotted back to third base after admonishing Cleon that he'd better get a hit.

So Cleon did. It was a home run over the left-field fence to assure the Mets' 11-6 victory. That's the kind of year it had been.

The Mets were jubilant as they flew back to New York that night, knowing only one more victory stood between them and the World Series. But Bud Harrelson did not join in the merrymaking. "Why are those guys laughing?" he asked a friend. "We haven't won a darn thing yet. The division means nothing. It's getting into the World Series that gets us the big money, and we've still got to win one more game to do that."

Harrelson was right. Under the new system, members of the losing team in the playoff were guaranteed at least $5,000 apiece. The winners got nothing from the playoff, but were guaranteed at least $10,000 apiece from the World Series. The World Series winners would get at least $15,000 each.

In the American League, the Minnesota Twins had lost their

first two games to Baltimore and also faced instant elimination in the playoffs. Bob (Righty) Miller was due to pitch the third game for Minnesota, and he had dreamed of the Twins winning three in a row so he could start a World Series game against his old teammates.

As the Braves prepared to come to New York, Henry Aaron recalled the 1958 World Series. The Braves, then making their temporary home in Milwaukee, trailed the Yankees three games to one in the best-of-seven series and won the next three to take it all. "It could happen again," Henry said wishfully.

The Braves came up with their third straight right-handed starting pitcher for the third game of the playoffs in Shea, and that meant Gil Hodges' lefty platoon would be back in action before 53,000 screaming fans with a chance to clinch it all this Monday afternoon.

Hodges' pitching choice, as determined by the season-long rotation, was Gary Gentry. Perhaps the rookie would finally succeed in giving the Mets a strong game. But the crazy pattern of the playoffs was continued in the very first inning. Gentry, like Seaver and Koosman in the first two games, knew he would have to be sustained by Met bats, if at all, when Tony Gonzalez singled and Aaron hit his third home run of the playoffs for a 2-0 Atlanta lead.

Gentry was far from sharp. He made it through the second inning, but in the third the Braves threatened again. Gonzalez led off with a single, and Aaron, who was having a magnificent series, followed with a double to left-center. None out, Braves on second and third, and the dangerous Rico Carty coming to bat with a chance to break the game wide open. Gentry, struggling, went to one ball and two strikes on Carty, and in the Braves' dugout Clete Boyer observed, "He's not throwing as hard as usual. We can hit him." On Gentry's fourth pitch, Carty took a vicious swing and whistled a line drive that traveled like a shot into the left-field corner before hooking safely wide of the foul pole and into the stands.

The crowd sighed in relief at the near-miss, then hummed with anticipation. Gil Hodges was on his way to the mound almost before Carty's drive reached the stands. Gentry, celebrating his twenty-third birthday, knew what was coming and glared at his approaching manager. "You're out of the game," Hodges said firmly and took the ball from the rookie. With a wave of his right arm, Hodges signaled for Nolan Ryan.

As Ryan, a twenty-two-year-old Texan, warmed up, Carty went to his dugout. "I don't know this guy. What does he throw?" the Braves outfielder asked.

"Fast balls and sliders," came the answer from various stations up and down the bench. Carty had never seen Ryan pitch. In 1968, the right-handed-hitting Dominican had been forced to spend the year in a sanitorium when it was discovered he had tuberculosis. This past season, as he battled to make his successful comeback, a combination of service calls and injuries had kept Ryan from ever pitching against the Braves.

Injuries and service calls, that had been the story of Nolan Ryan's pitching career. Even in high school, the skinny 6-1, 158-pounder had trouble with blisters, and he was unmercifully overworked by the coach at Alvin High in his senior season. Through that final year, he worked 159 innings, more than many pros, and scouts who saw him worn out late in the season were unimpressed. That's why he was still available for the Mets to grab him as the 295th player selected in the 1965 draft. To celebrate being chosen by the Mets, he went out and fanned twelve in a no-hitter.

After signing with the Mets for about $10,000, Ryan struck out 115 batters in 78 innings in a rookie league. The following year, 1966, he fanned 313 in 205 innings for three clubs, including a brief visit with the Mets. Baseball experts figure a ratio of one strikeout per inning is exceptional. Ryan's figures were unbelievable.

Ryan was conceded a good chance to make the Mets in 1967, but he had gone into the service and blew the first half of the season. Then, when the Mets were ready to call him up from Jacksonville after he had returned from the army and had pitched himself into shape, he hurt his elbow while warming up on the sidelines the day before he was to report to New York. That finished the second half of the season.

When Ryan finally reported to the Mets in the spring of 1968, the players were awed by his reputation. He was a legend before his own time, and in the Saint Petersburg clubhouse they jokingly called him "Myth Ryan." The big gag was to pretend there really was no Nolan Ryan. When a veteran did engage the rookie in conversation, his teammates would ask incredulously, "Why are you standing there talking to yourself?"

Blisters continued to plague Ryan through his rookie season, and Gus Mauch, the Met trainer, finally hit on a solution after all his

First in the National League. From left, Ken Boswell,
Tommie Agee, Nolan Ryan, and Wayne Garrett celebrate
after completing their sweep of the Braves.
Boswell, Agee, and Garrett hit home runs;
Ryan turned in an outstanding relief job.

salves and modern medications had failed. He stopped off at a
kosher delicatessen near his apartment in the Bronx and, for a few
cents, purchased a container of pickle brine. Mauch's prescription
was for Ryan to soak his finger in the brine to toughen the skin.
It worked, but Ryan wouldn't continue the remedy. What does a
boy out of Alvin, Texas, know from kosher pickles? "I can't stand
the smell," he complained, and got blisters.

After the blisters, and that arm trouble, Ryan also developed a
tendency to pull his groin muscles. Some players throw hard enough
to hurt muscles in their arms or shoulders; Ryan got his whole body
behind his fast ball and pulled the groin muscles. With the injuries, plus his regular tours with a reserve unit, Ryan was able to
appear in only 89 innings for the 1969 Mets. But he struck out 92
batters. Red Murff, who had scouted him, liked to say Ryan threw
"bees at the knees." In the players' vernacular, Ryan threw "nothing
but smoke." The Mets needed smoke today. Right now.

The crowd stilled as Carty moved into the batter's box and Ryan took his place on the mound and looked in for the sign. He really needn't have bothered. Everybody in the ball park knew what he was going to throw. The Mets needed a strikeout. And what was Ryan's strikeout pitch? Jerry Grote, who, like Gentry, was celebrating a birthday, his twenty-seventh, squatted behind the plate and began flashing his fingers in the sequence of signs. The code spelled out fast ball, and Ryan delivered the mail, special delivery. The pitch whistled past Carty's flailing bat and Ryan had his strikeout. "Only one man could have struck Carty out in that situation," said Paul Richards, boss of the Braves, as he marveled at Hodges' ability once again to make the perfect tactical move. "He has to strike Carty out or we play again tomorrow."

With Carty disposed of, the Mets could now maneuver. Orlando Cepeda was walked to fill the bases and to set up a possible double play. Then Ryan drilled a called third strike past Clete Boyer and got Bob Didier on a fly to left. The Mets were out of the inning.

As the Braves took the field, they had to know they were on their way out of the playoffs despite their two-run lead. Tommie Agee hit a home run in the bottom of the third and Ken Boswell, one of the Mets' newer hitting heroes, slammed a two-run homer over the right-field fence in the fourth. Even though the Braves went back in front by a run on Cepeda's two-run homer in the fifth, it was only a matter of time. The Mets were a team of destiny. "They hear voices," columnist Milton Gross wrote, and he wasn't very wrong.

Leading off the home half of the fifth, Ryan, who had managed only three hits all season for a .103 average, bounced a single to right, and red-haired Wayne Garrett, drafted for $25,000 from those very same Braves, hit his first home run in five months—and only his second of the year—to put the Mets ahead for good. With Ryan allowing only three hits and fanning seven in as many innings, the Mets completed their sweep with a 7-4 victory.

They were champions, not of some bobtailed Eastern Division, but of the whole National League, and once again their fans poured out on the field.

And less than two minutes after Garrett threw out Gonzalez to end the game and touch off the madness, at nearby Belmont Park race track a four-year-old colt named The University won the first division of the Long Island Handicap by a nose. The horse, owned by the Greentree Stable of Mrs. Payson and her brother,

Jock Whitney, paid 10-to-1. The Mets were a longer price than that.

The opposition best eulogized the Mets' achievement.

"They beat the hell out of us," said Luman Harris, manager of the defeated Braves.

"You could send the Mets to Vietnam and they'd end it in three days," said Paul Richards, the losing general manager who no longer could scoff at the Mets' untouchables.

"They are amazing," said Henry Aaron, a pretty amazing guy himself.

And over in the American League, the Baltimore Orioles swept Minnesota in three games to win their pennant and set up the World Series pairings. Oddsmakers quickly installed the Mets as underdogs again. The price was 8-to-5.

16

Mrs. Duffy's Banner

Frank Robinson wants to be a manager, and a manager plays a baseball game of fifty men, not twenty-five or eighteen or nine. That may have been why the Oriole outfielder was staring over at the Met dugout as the National League champions batted in the seventh inning of the first World Series game in Baltimore's Memorial Stadium on Saturday, October 11.

The Mets, trailing, 4-0, had a rally started. Donn Clendenon led off with a single, Ron Swoboda walked, and with one out, Jerry Grote singled to load the bases. The tying run was at the plate in the person of occasional hero Al Weis when Frank Robinson thought he saw an omen. "They're not cheering," he said in wonderment. "They've got a chance to get back in the ball game and there's no enthusiasm." And Frank Robinson smiled his little half smile even though Weis did deliver a sacrifice fly for one run.

The inning wasn't over, but soon it became the Orioles' turn to cheer. Rod Gaspar, batting for the pitcher, topped a tricky little trickler between third and the pitcher's mound. Rod Gaspar can run and he was doing what he did best, speeding toward first base. But Brooks Robinson, the Orioles' All-Star third-baseman, was doing what he did best, too. Flying in, he scooped the ball barehanded and, with one motion, fired on to first base to retire Gaspar, end the inning, finish the Mets in a 4-1 defeat, and give the favored Orioles that important first-game advantage in the Series. "Not one third-baseman in a hundred would have been able to make that play, but Brooks Robinson is one third-baseman in a million," Leonard Koppett wrote in the *New York Times*.

146

Trading for Donn Clendenon made a difference.

"We are here to prove there is no Santa Claus," Brooks Robinson had said during batting practice, and he played Scrooge all by himself against the popular favorites that afternoon.

It was just one of those awful days for the Mets. No wonder Frank Robinson had detected a note of apathy.

It all began at breakfast. Or at breakfast time. Tom Seaver, the Mets' scheduled starting pitcher, went down to the hotel coffee-shop only to be warned by his roomie, Bud Harrelson, "Better forget it. I've been here twenty minutes and I haven't seen a waiter yet." Tom Seaver is a well-regulated young man. He sleeps a certain number of hours (twelve) two nights before a game in which he is to start and a certain number (nine) on the eve of his assignment. His diet is adjusted to the pitching rotation, too. Tom Seaver's schedule does not include skipping breakfast on the day he is supposed to pitch. A thin, dry roast-beef sandwich in the clubhouse before his warmups was no substitute.

If Seaver was less than ready when the game started, he was awakened in a hurry. Don Buford, who had preceded Tom at Southern Cal, hit his second pitch, an inside fast ball, over the fence in right field for a home run. It didn't go over the fence by much, just enough.

Ron Swoboda, playing for the first time in eight days, was in right field for the Mets. The Orioles were starting a southpaw, Mike Cuellar, which meant that Gil Hodges' lefty platoon, which had swept the Braves, was being benched. Swoboda was starting in right in place of Art Shamsky. Ron is from Baltimore, and as he went out to his position he thought about how he had played in this stadium in high school. As Buford hit what appeared to be a routine fly, Swoboda backed easily against the canvas-covered fence. As he saw the ball would just clear the fence, Swoboda leaped to grab it, but his back hit the barrier on the way up and the ball grazed off the top of his glove. Home run.

Another fly ball, this one hit almost a week earlier, began to take its toll on Seaver in the fourth inning. The day after he had staggered to victory in the first playoff game against the Braves, Seaver was in the outfield shagging flies during batting practice. Jerry Koosman hit a line drive, in itself a noteworthy occurrence, and Seaver strained a muscle in his left calf making the catch. From that day, he did no running in the outfield. Take away breakfast, take away his usual conditioning program, and Seaver's legs began to grow weary in the fourth inning.

With two out, he collapsed. Elrod Hendricks singled, **Dave Johnson** walked, Mark Belanger singled for one run, Mike Cuellar singled for another, and then Buford doubled for another. The Orioles had a 4-0 lead and, except for Buford, the damage had been done by ping hitters Seaver should have been able to retire left-handed.

Seaver finally got the side out, and then came another scoreless inning before Hodges began leafing through his pinch-hitters. But the game was lost, and the Mets' malaise wasn't helped by the crowd. Only 50,429 paid in, more than 2,000 less than capacity. Why, the Mets drew that many at Shea for batting practice! What's with these Oriole fans?

Perhaps those fans had been spoiled by success and the prospect of an easy Oriole victory in the World Series. The Birds had run away with the title in the American League East by winning 109 games, a major-league high, and then swept aside Minnesota in the playoff three straight. This was a team of super stars: Boog Powell with his thirty-seven home runs on first base and perennial All-Star Brooks Robinson on third flanked a pair of .280-hitting whippets up the middle, Mark Belanger and Dave Johnson, for a standout infield. Frank Robinson hit thirty-two home runs, drove in a hundred runs, and batted .308 to lead an outfield that also included fleet Don Buford and even speedier Paul Blair, who hit twenty-six home runs. The pitching staff was led by two twenty-game winners, Mike Cuellar (23-11) and Dave McNally (20-7), and the No. 3 starter, Jim Palmer, was 16-and-4. Only behind the plate did Earl Weaver, Baltimore's feisty little manager, have to platoon.

Against this array, what did the Mets have to offer but a couple of pitchers and only one real hitter, Cleon Jones, who still had to establish a permanent reputation? If the pitching faltered, as it did in the playoffs and the Series opener, it would be no contest. If this were football, the team from Baltimore might have been an 18-point favorite over the team from New York.

Shockingly, there again were 2,000 or more empty seats when the Orioles and Mets went at it in the second game. Maybe the good Baltimoreans were home celebrating Columbus Day. This time the omens were on the Mets' side. Jerry Koosman, their starting pitcher, got breakfast and, it's nice to believe, an inspirational boost because his son, like Columbus, was celebrating a birthday. (Michael Scott Koosman was two.) And the Orioles suffered a pre-game fright when Frank Robinson, who had led them to a pennant and a World Series sweep in 1966, fouled a baseball off his left instep in batting practice. Robinson played, but in pain.

Back at the Mets' hotel in the last hours before game time, Mrs. Duffy Dyer, wife of the third-string catcher, stripped the sheet off their bed and commenced daubing at it with some black shoe polish. The Mets would not be lethargic on this Sunday afternoon. Among other things, they had read some of Frank Robinson's comments on their lack of spirit in the morning press.

Koosman was sharp today. He zipped the Orioles for three straight innings, and then Donn Clendenon hit a home run in the fourth as Mrs. Payson almost jumped into the dugout from her adjacent field-level seat. And after he finished applauding Clendenon's blow, Koosman went out and zipped the Orioles for three more innings.

For six innings, Jerry Koosman, the farm boy from Minnesota, had a no-hitter, thanks to a diving catch of Buford's line drive by Bud Harrelson in the third. But he only had a 1-0 lead as McNally, another left-hander, almost matched him pitch for pitch.

Paul Blair, the swift center-fielder who had once been a Met farm hand before the Orioles snatched him in the draft for a mere $8,000, led off Baltimore's seventh with a single to left. The blow eased the no-hit pressure but provided Koosman with more immediate problems. This was a very close ball game, a game he could lose. Forget those childhood dreams of pitching a World Series no-hitter, Jerry had to tell himself. The Met lefty got Frank Robinson on a fly ball to center, and then ponderous Boog Powell lifted a pop fly to short. As the ball was descending, second-baseman Al Weis screamed at Bud Harrelson to let it drop. That way the Mets could force Blair at second and replace him as a base-runner with the slow-footed Powell. However, Harrelson elected to catch the ball. He had noticed he was on the dirt portion of the infield, and he feared a bad bounce if he let the ball hit. The decision cost him. Powell was out and Blair stole second, something Boog couldn't have done with an 80-foot lead. Now in scoring position, it was easy for Blair to tally on Brooks Robinson's single. The score was tied.

With the no-hit pressure on her husband's teammate removed, Mrs. Duffy Dyer jumped to her feet in the less-than-desirable right-field seats that had been allotted to Met wives. She unfurled her bed sheet, which the black shoe polish had transformed into a banner bearing the classic exhortation: "Let's Go Mets." Mrs. Nolan Ryan, Mrs. Tom Seaver, and Mrs. Bobby Pfeil volunteered to grab a corner and they were off. For several delicious minutes between innings, Memorial Stadium acquired the madness of Shea as the four pretty young ladies paraded down the aisle with their banner. Their husbands saw and were secretly delighted, especially when they learned the deed had upset their opponents. "We've pulled stunts like painting the other team's bullpen, but at least I didn't bring my wife to carry the paint bucket," Baltimore pitcher Pete Richert grumbled. (Of all people to complain, really. Richert is from Long Island, home base of the Shea nonsense. He should have understood, but, then, Pete Richert is a left-hander. Anyway, he got his before the Series ended, but that's another chapter.)

It took a full inning for their wives' enthusiastic display to affect the Mets. It was now the top of the ninth, and McNally, who had given up only three hits to the righty platoon, was going strong. He got Clendenon and Swoboda for the first two outs, but then Ed Charles singled to left. Jerry Grote did the same, and Charles went to third on his thirty-six-year-old legs. That brought up Al Weis, the .215 hitter, and left both managers with some decisions to ponder. Hodges, of course, could call on a pinch-hitter with more threatening credentials. Weaver had two alternatives. He had to decide whether to relieve McNally and then he had to choose whether to pitch to Weis or walk him intentionally and bring up Koosman, a feeble batter whose first major-league hit the season before had inspired a champagne party. (If Hodges then pinch-hit for Koosman, Weaver at least would have forced the Mets' second-best pitcher out of the game.)

Both managers, however, elected to play with a pat hand. Hodges stayed with Weis and Weaver stayed with McNally, giving him orders to get the little infielder out. Perhaps Weaver would have acted differently if he had known that McNally was one of only six pitchers in all big-league baseball who had ever given up a home run to Al Weis. Of course, there were many more times he had not given up a home run to Al Weis, and so the odds were really pretty good. The odds also were pretty good against McNally's throwing a bad pitch. You don't go 20-and-7 throwing many bad pitches, but on this day and at this moment, Dave McNally hung a slider. His eyes wide at such good fortune, Al Weis hit a line drive to left for the go-ahead run.

There was still the last of the ninth, though, and Koosman had to protect his slim lead against the top of the Oriole batting order, the men who were supposed to give Baltimore such a big edge. The pressure-proof left-hander retired Buford and Blair for the first two outs, and now it was Frank Robinson coming up, dangerous as a wounded cat, his left foot throbbing from the pre-game injury.

At this point, Hodges called on a tactic he had used before against some of the National League's dangerous power hitters like Willie McCovey and Richie Allen. With the bases empty and the Mets tied or ahead by one run, Hodges would station his second-baseman in left field near the foul line. The other outfielders would shade over, providing a deep umbrella defense. The right side of the infield was open. The object, of course, was to cut down the possibility of an extra-base hit. If Frank Robinson singled, it would still take two more singles to bring him home, quite unlikely with two men out.

Frank Robinson did end up on first, but not according to blue-print. Koosman walked him on a 3-and-2 pitch, and the fielders returned to their normal alignment. The situation was uncomfortable but not yet desperate until Koosman followed by going 3-and-2 on Boog Powell and walking him, too. Hodges didn't hesitate. He called in Ron Taylor, the right-handed, Canadian-born electrical engineer. Taylor, who had undergone complicated back surgery to save his baseball career, was the Mets' best relief pitcher. His assignment from Hodges as he came in to face Brooks Robinson: "Get this man out."

Taylor's first two pitches were out of the strike zone, and this gave the gentlemanly Oriole the upper hand. Brooks took a strike but then Taylor threw another ball, and again the advantage went to the batter. Taylor had no more pitches to play with. The time for finesse was over. He had to go with his best pitch, a sinking fast ball, and Robinson beat it into the ground toward third. The ball smacked off Charles' chest, and the poet picked it up and turned toward third, hoping to get the final out on a force play without risking a throw. Merv Rettenmund was running for the hobbled Frank Robinson and he was too close to the bag. Charles couldn't risk losing a foot race, so he turned and fired hastily to first. The throw was low, into the dirt, but Clendenon dug it out. Brooks Robinson can do everything—everything but run. He was out by two steps. "The story of my life," he said resignedly afterward. The Mets had won, 2-1, and they would be returning to their home ball park all even at a game apiece.

17

"The Impossible Dream" Comes True

After a day off for travel, devoted to workouts by both teams in the new venue, the Mets were back in their element, which translates into a jam-packed, hysterical stadium screaming unanimous support of the home team. Jackie Kennedy Onassis and her children and her new husband were included in the throng (he left early) along with numerous celebrities, several hundred Vietnam veterans, and thousands of the New Breed finally enjoying some of that old-fashioned success.

Of the 56,335 fans in Shea Stadium on this overcast Tuesday, the millions watching on television, and the millions more listening on radio, nobody would be paying closer attention to the day's activities than the student body at the Mobile County Training School just outside Mobile, Alabama. Cleon Jones and Tommie Agee of the Mets are two of the school's most famous alumni (Billy Williams of the Cubs makes it three graduates in the majors), and R. A. Holt, the principal, wondered how his students could concentrate on their studies while the World Series was going on. Wisely, Holt bowed to the inevitable. Classes would be suspended during the World Series games. The inspiration of what Agee and Jones had been able to achieve despite origins as humble as any of the students' was justification enough for Holt's decision. Besides, he doubled as the school's athletic coach. He wanted to see the games himself.

What these students saw in the third World Series game was one of the greatest one-man shows in the history of the post-season

154

Tommie Agee makes his great catch on Elrod Hendricks as Cleon Jones watches.

competition. Seldom had a nonpitcher so dominated nine innings of World Series baseball.

Gary Gentry started for the Mets and Jim Palmer pitched for the Orioles, which gave Hodges' left-handed platoon a chance to play. The Mets wasted little time in showing how glad they were to return home. Leading off the first inning, Agee smashed a 2-and-1 pitch over the fence in left center, the fifth time this year he had started a game with a home run.

The bottom half of the Mets' lineup produced two more runs in the second. With two out, Jerry Grote walked, Bud Harrelson singled him to third, and then Gentry, who had driven in only one run all season, ended an 0-for-28 slump by driving Palmer's first pitch to right center for a two-run double. Paul Blair and Frank Robinson (X rays had showed his foot was not broken) looked at each other in shocked disbelief as the ball sailed over their heads.

Gentry retired ten of the first eleven Baltimore batters, but with two out in the fourth, Elrod Hendricks came up with two men on base. Agee was playing him toward right field in accordance with the Mets' scouting report when the left-handed-hitting Virgin Islander smashed a long fly toward the wall in left center. Jones had no chance on it, but Agee took off at full speed as if he were still running the hundred in 9.7 for Mobile County Training School. He raced over the uneven outfield, reached high across his body, and picked off the ball backhanded in the webbing of his glove two feet from the 396-foot marker on the wall. "Plenty of room," Jones had been yelling, an acceptable deception under the circumstances.

The Mets added another run in the sixth to go ahead, 4-0, but the Orioles were making threatening noises in the seventh. With two out, Gentry walked the bases loaded and then he took a walk himself as Hodges summoned Nolan Ryan from the bullpen.

Ryan had rescued the Mets with one pitch in the playoffs, but this time he had to work a little harder. He had an 0-and-2 count on Paul Blair when the Orioles' center-fielder lashed a line drive to right center. With two out, the runners were going and all would score on the certain extra-base hit. But Agee was barreling across the outfield again, and this time he was more confident than on his previous catch against Hendricks. He even tapped his glove in assurance before realizing with a shock that a gust of wind off Flushing Bay was carrying the ball down and away from him. In desperation he threw himself at the ball and caught it diving on his belly toward the warning track.

Ed Kranepool hit a ninth-inning home run, and Ryan completed the 5-0 victory, but the day belonged to Agee. He had saved two runs with his catch in the fourth and three more with his catch in the seventh. Give the Orioles those five runs, take away Agee's own homer and Baltimore wins, 5-4. But the game is played with "ifs" only in saloons in the wintertime. The Mets now held a 2-to-1 advantage in games.

There were crowds outside Shea Stadium early before the fourth game, but not all the people were baseball fans. This was the day of the first Vietnam Moratorium, October 15, and youths wearing black armbands handed out leaflets to the early arrivals. A picture of Tom Seaver decorated many of them.

"If the Mets can win the World Series, why can't we end the war in Vietnam?" the leaflets quoted Seaver, who had promised to make a public statement to that effect after the Series. Without asking Tom, the pamphleteers had jumped the gun. Seaver was due to pitch that afternoon, and the unauthorized use of his picture on the leaflets angered him. "As an American citizen, I'm entitled to my opinions," he said, but he didn't like being exploited for those opinions.

One protester, however, with an eye on both worlds, carried a sign reading, "Bomb the Orioles, not the peasants."

Inside the stadium it was Seaver and Mike Cuellar, the first-game antagonists, and this time the Mets got an early home-run jump when Donn Clendenon hit one in the second inning.

After Clendenon's home run had brought a roar from the record paying Shea crowd of 57,367, Earl Weaver, Baltimore's aggressive manager, seemed to believe his team needed inspiration, since none of their wives had volunteered to parade a banner through the stands. So with Mark Belanger, the leadoff batter in the next inning, at the plate, Weaver charged out to protest a strike call and was banished by the plate umpire, Shag Crawford, a National Leaguer. World Series or no, a manager who argues a strike call is automatically ejected, and Crawford was inflexible. Weaver thus became only the third manager in history and the first in thirty-four years to be thrown out of a World Series game.

The Orioles needed more than inspiration, though. Seaver was more than making up for his two poor postseason games. He gave up a hit in the first inning and two more in the third, and then he retired nineteen of twenty batters into the ninth. Then, with one down, Frank Robinson singled to left and went all the way to third despite his painful foot as Boog Powell singled to right. Up came Brooks Robinson, a dependable clutch hitter, and Gil Hodges walked slowly to the mound. "Look," he reminded Seaver, "if the ball is hit to you, don't take a chance and try for the double play, go right home with it. I don't want the tying run scoring."

As Brooks Robinson came to bat, Ron Swoboda in right edged some 20 feet toward the infield. His play, too, was to cut down the tying run at the plate. As Swoboda moved in, the batter sent a searing line drive to his barehanded side. By cheating toward the infield, Swoboda had made it impossible to play the ball safe and cut it off for a single. It was extra bases any way he looked at it, and he couldn't stop to think. Acting on instinct, the hulking outfielder raced several steps to his right and dived at the ball, his body horizontal less than a foot off the ground, his glove hand straining. The line drive smacked into the webbing of his glove as he hit the ground, rolled over, and came up minus his cap but with the ball. Frank Robinson was able to lope home with the tying run, but Swoboda's catch had provided an out and prevented any further advance. Swoboda, he of the iron hands and jerky movements, had been anointed with the other Mets. "Is God a Met?" Sandy Koufax had asked Tom Seaver jokingly during the National League playoffs.

"No, but I believe he has an apartment in New York," the pitcher had answered. Swoboda, once the outfield clown, suddenly was one with Tommie Agee and Tris Speaker.

Another out and the Orioles were finished in the ninth. The Mets threatened but failed to score in their half, and the Orioles made some noises against Seaver in the tenth but left a couple of runners on base. This, Gil Hodges decided to himself, would be Seaver's last inning.

The Mets, of little reputation but recent fame, took over in the last of the tenth. Leading off, Jerry Grote hit a fly ball to left that Don Buford misjudged into a double and Rod Gaspar came in to run for him. "Who in hell is Ron [sic] Gaspar?" the Orioles had gibed as they watched the Met rookie cavort on TV after the playoff sweep. Soon they would find out. Silent Al Weis, next up, was walked intentionally, and J. C. Martin batted for Seaver.

Everybody in the ball park knew Martin's assignment was to lay down a sacrifice bunt, preferably toward third so the third-baseman would have to desert his position to field it and thus assure the advance of the winning run. Baltimore already had used three pitchers, and now Billy Hunter, acting as manager for the absent Weaver, signaled in a fourth, southpaw Pete Richert, to oppose the lefty-swinging Martin.

Richert got quite a workout for his brief exposure. He threw one pitch and Martin bunted it out to the left of the mound. Richert came flying in to pounce on the ball, oblivious of catcher Elrod Hendricks screaming, "I've got it, I've got it." The catcher would have been in a better position for a throw to first, the only play, but

Gil Hodges shows umpire Lou DiMuro the spot on the ball.

Richert didn't hear. He grabbed the ball and, as a left-hander, had to pivot all the way around to throw to first. Dave Johnson, the second-baseman, was covering. As Martin lumbered down the line as fast as his catcher's legs would take him, he could tell from Johnson's movements where the ball was coming. He tried to "swell up"—like a frog—and veered to the inside of the baseline, an infraction that's never called and which was never noticed until postgame photographs made it obvious. Running with his arms outstretched, Martin was a foot from the bag when the ball caromed off his left wrist—raising a "happy knob," he said later—and rolled off between first and second. As Johnson scampered to retrieve the ball, Eddie Yost, coaching at third base, was screaming at Gaspar to keep running. Finally, the rookie got the message and loped home without a play, his left foot stamping emphatically on the plate as if to seal officially the 2-1 victory.*

The Mets had won, and for the first time the Orioles seemed to sense the inevitability of defeat. "If the throw was good, I'd probably have caught it, but I'd have been trampled and I would have laid there with the ball in my hand while the run scored," Dave Johnson said fatalistically.

"It looked," said Ron Swoboda, who had initiated a good many of those Three Stooges comedies himself over the years, "like a Chinese fire drill."

The Mets, after losing the first game, now were within one victory of clinching the world championship. Jerry Koosman would be their pitcher, and he reminded all in the clubhouse, "Remember, I predicted we'd win in four straight. I didn't say the first four, I predicted four straight," he shouted before adding in more subdued tones, almost to himself, "Tomorrow the impossible dream comes true."

It looked as if the impossible might be delayed awhile as 57,397 —thirty more than the previous day's record—jammed Shea Stadium for the potential clincher.

In the third inning, Mark Belanger hit a single, Dave McNally, who was opposing Koosman again, hit a home run, and then Frank Robinson hit a home run for a 3-0 lead. Travel representatives

---

* As an oddity, the winning run in each of the first four games was accounted for by a man who had been traded away by the Chicago White Sox: Don Buford for the Orioles; Al Weis, Tommie Agee, and J. C. Martin for the Mets.

How sweet it is! Ron Swoboda embraces Tommie Agee
as Cleon Jones brings up the rear.

started canvassing the long press area to see which writers would
require transportation to Baltimore for the sixth game of the Series.

The Mets, however, were not booking passage, especially not to
any place as nonterrestrial as Baltimore.

They finally began to rally in the sixth, with Cleon Jones literally
kicking it off by failing to skip out of the way of a McNally curve

ball into the dirt. The pitch skidded off into the Met dugout as Lou DiMuro, the plate umpire, almost automatically clicked off "ball" on the little indicator he held in his palm. But slowly Gil Hodges emerged from the dugout, carrying a baseball and calling for time. Patiently, he showed the ball to DiMuro, who, after a short pause, waved Cleon Jones on to first base. This is what happened: Jones had claimed the ball had hit him on the foot. Baseball players' game shoes are freshly shined every day. Hodges was showing DiMuro the baseball clearly marked with a smudge of shoe polish. Verdict to the complainant. Case closed.

(Ironically, in the top half of the sixth, Frank Robinson had been hit on the left thigh by a pitch, but DiMuro had ruled in this case the ball had glanced off Robinson's bat before hitting him. Robinson required first aid in the dugout, but to no avail. His only consolation was that movies subsequently showed he had been entitled to first base.)

"You always keep a few baseballs with shoe polish on them in the dugout," Casey Stengel chortled as he recalled a World Series game a dozen years ago. Another Jones, Vernal (Nippy) Jones, was playing for Milwaukee against Stengel's Yankees, and he got to first base on just such a shoe-polish-appeal play. Later in that inning, Eddie Mathews had hit a game-winning home run.

History repeated with a thunderclap. Donn Clendenon, next up after Jones, hit a 2-2 pitch into the stands in left. It was his third homer of the series, one short of the World Series record. (Adding Ed Kranepool's homer in the third game, the Mets showed four homers from the one position.)

Clendenon's home run cut Baltimore's lead to 3-2, and in the next inning Al Weis smacked a game-tying homer over the wall in left. It was the first home run he'd hit in Shea Stadium during two years as a Met and only his third of the year. It also gave McNally the dubious distinction of being the only man in baseball, majors or minors, to have had Al Weis hit two home runs off him. "I knew I hit it good, but I didn't know how far it was going to go. I don't have enough experience in judging those things," Weis confessed later.

Any confidence the Orioles retained of bringing the Series back to Baltimore seemed to go out of them with Weis's home run. Koosman was getting stronger and, in the last of the eighth, Cleon Jones doubled and scored the go-ahead run on a double by Ron Swo-

Met fans go on a tear after their glorious victory.

boda. And then Swoboda scored an insurance run when the Orioles committed a double error on Jerry Grote's ground ball to wrap up the 5-3 victory.

As the Mets became World Champions—winning four straight as Jerry Koosman had predicted—it was almost as if the spirit of their past ineptitude was being transferred into other bodies. The Mets would live, not only in memory, but in a dropped fly ball here, a booted grounder there, and somebody missing first base—and second—somewhere else. But after all, who wants to live in a world where everybody's perfect?

18

Epilogue to a Summer of Joy

The supper club in Caesar's Palace in gaudy Las Vegas turned dark. The music was from *Man of La Mancha*. But the words? And those voices?

> "*. . . This was our quest*
> *To fight as a team*
> *No matter how hopeless*
> *The struggle may seem. . . .*
> *And we knew*
> *If we'd only be true*
> *To this glorious quest*
> *That the flag would belong to our team,*
> *To a team that is blessed.*"

The lights flashed on and there was comedian Phil Foster introducing Met heroes Tommie Agee, Donn Clendenon, Cleon Jones, Jerry Koosman, Ed Kranepool, Tom Seaver, and Art Shamsky.

This was one of the more glamorous payoffs of the Mets' magnificent achievement. Each of the seven players received $10,000 for the two-week engagement in Las Vegas, and if they didn't make any lasting contribution to the art of song, dance, and comedy, they didn't inflict any permanent damage, either.

Two other Mets had been invited to join this troupe, but they had more compelling commitments. Ron Swoboda had agreed to tour military hospitals in the Pacific and Far East, and Ed Charles was making a similar tour in Vietnam. Honor dictated that they decline Las Vegas, and it was a special sacrifice for Charles. This would be the last turn on baseball's merry-go-round for The Glider, his last chance at any brass rings.

Of course, there were other goodies for the winners—prizes, endorsements, speaking engagements, off-season jobs, big raises for 1970. Donn Clendenon received the *Sport* magazine sports car as the most valuable player in the World Series, plus a voluntary salary adjustment from the Mets. (He had come to them after signing a two-year contract with the Expos which was still in effect.) A Brooklyn auto dealer thought Al Weis had been slighted in the voting, so he appropriately gave the little infielder a Volkswagen for consolation.

Gil Hodges, everybody's Manager of the Year, was awarded a new contract by the club as he completed the second season of a three-year contract at $57,000 a year. The Mets gave him a bonus for 1969 and then wrote a new three-year deal at $70,000 per.

John Murphy, the general manager, was named Executive of the Year by *Sporting News,* and Tom Seaver was a runaway choice for the Cy Young Award as the National League's best pitcher.

All Mets shared in a record World Series payoff of $18,338.18 per man, almost $5,500 more than the previous high. Thirty-five full shares were voted by the players, including one to Bobby Pfeil, the infielder whose glove, at least, got into the World Series. Because they had been bringing up extra players to fill in during weekend and two-week service tours of their regular cast, the Mets found themselves at the end of the season with twenty-six men eligible for the playoffs and World Series. The limit was twenty-five, and on the eve of the playoffs, Hodges tabbed Pfeil as the most expendable. However, the Mets took Bobby along as a member of their official party all the way to the World Series conclusion. And during the Series, M. Donald Grant carried Pfeil's glove as insurance in case any foul balls came whistling too close to Mrs. Payson's box seat.

But the end of one season really means only the beginning of another.

As the players were still figuring out how to spend their World Series money, Murphy and Hodges huddled to assure that there might be more fat checks to divide in 1970. Young prospects had to be protected from the draft and helpful deals could be made while Met players still had that sought-after world-champion image.

The World Champions are showered with ticker tape
as they ride up Broadway en route to a City Hall reception.

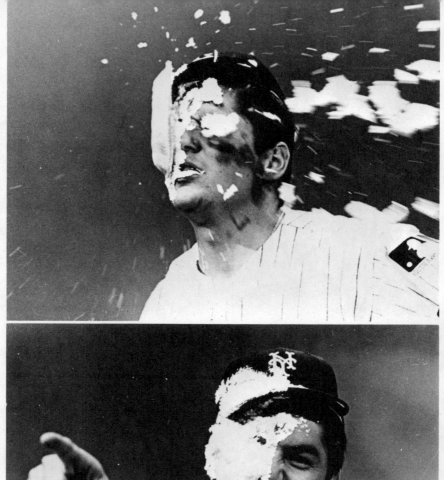
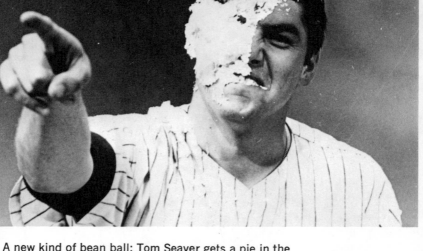

A new kind of bean ball: Tom Seaver gets a pie in the
face rehearsing for a TV appearance.

From Kansas City, Murphy obtained Joe Foy, a Bronx lad who, he hoped, would finally end the long parade at third base. No fewer than forty-one different men had played third for the Mets since their birth, and six had taken at least one turn at the position in 1969. To get Foy, Murphy surrendered one of those six, Amos Otis, the former untouchable, and Bob Johnson, a righty pitcher. Both had spent most of the season in the minors.

Then Murphy picked up veteran lefty Ray Sadecki, as insurance for his already-strong pitching staff, and outfielder Dave Marshall from the Giants for two more farm hands who had enjoyed the briefest of visits at Shea Stadium in 1969, outfielder Jim Gosger and infielder Bob Heise.

During the winter meetings, Jack DiLauro, who had been dropped to the Tidewater farm-team roster, was drafted by Houston, who figured a castoff Met still might be able to help them even if they had beaten New York ten of twelve times during the 1969 season.

In South Bend, Indiana, Notre Dame's football team accepted its first bid to a post-season game, the Cotton Bowl, in many years. However, one of its reserve ends, Nick Furlong, wouldn't be going with them. A starting pitcher for the Fighting Irish baseball team, Furlong elected to sign a contract with the Mets. Pitching, that's how champions are built and maintained.

At the time DiLauro was dropped, Ed Charles was given his unconditional release. The Mets felt his career as a player was over. However, they wanted him to remain with the organization and immediately offered him a job in their promotion department.

Although he felt he could still play major-league ball, Charles accepted the position and reported for work. But then he and Murphy got into an argument over their financial agreement. Charles said he had been promised moving expenses, Murphy denied it. Bitter and angry, Charles departed for his Kansas City home, vowing to get another playing job. Murphy repeated that the front-office position with the Mets was still open to him.

The courtly Murphy was deeply hurt by Charles' charges. He hoped for a reconciliation, but it was not to be. As the new year began, Murphy suffered his second heart attack within weeks and passed away. It was a shocking and unhappy ending to the glory year of 1969, but it would never erase the rapture of those September and October miracles and the thrilling days that led up to them.

When New York Mayor John V. Lindsay greeted the Mets at City Hall after a tumultuous victory parade, he told them, "Thank you for our summer of joy."

The memory of that "summer of joy" would always remain alive and glowing for Ed Charles, and his teammates, and baseball fans everywhere . . . including those newcomers to the fanatic ranks who found themselves magically caught up in that amazing whirlwind.

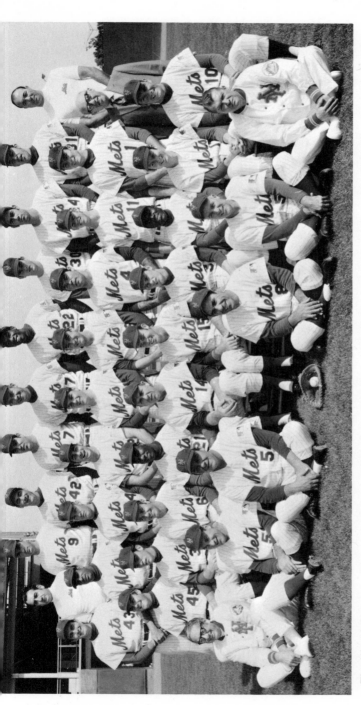

The World Champs: Front row (left to right): Gus Mauch, trainer; Joe Pignatano, coach; Rube Walker, coach; Yogi Berra, coach; Ed Yost, coach; Joe Deer, assistant trainer. Second row: Frank McGraw, Gary Gentry, Al Weis, Cleon Jones, Manager Gil Hodges, Jerry Grote, Bud Harrelson, Ed Charles, Rod Gaspar, Don Dyer. Third row: Jim McAndrew, Tommie Agee, Cal Koonce, Ken Boswell, Tom Seaver, Jerry Koosman, Ron Swoboda, Wayne Garrett, Bobby Pfeil, Lou Niss, traveling secretary. Back row: Nick Torman, equipment manager; J. C. Martin, Ron Taylor, Ed Kranepool, Don Cardwell, Donn Clendenon, Nolan Ryan, Art Shamsky, Jack DiLauro, Roy Neuer, club-house attendant.

All-Time Met
Roster and
Records

All-Time Met Roster

Agee, Tommie   1968-69
Alomar, Sandy   1967
Altman, George   1964
Anderson, Craig   1962-64
Arrigo, Gerry   1966
Ashburn, Richie   1962
Bauta, Ed   1963-64
Bearnarth, Larry   1963-66
Bell, Gus   1962
Bennett, Dennis   1967
Berra, Yogi   1965
Bethke, Jim   1965
Bosch, Don   1967-68
Boswell, Ken   1967-69
Bouchee, Ed   1962
Boyer, Ken   1966-67
Bressoud, Ed   1966
Buchek, Jerry   1967-68
Burright, Larry   1963-64
Cannizzaro, Chris   1962-65
Cardwell, Don   1967-69
Carmel, Duke   1963
Chacon, Elio   1962
Charles, Ed   1967-69
Chiti, Harry   1962
Christopher, Joe   1962-65
Cisco, Galen   1962-65
Clendenon, Donn   1969
Coleman, Clarence   1962-63, 1965
Collins, Kevin   1965, 1967-69
Connors, Bill   1967-68
Cook, Cliff   1962-63
Cowan, Billy   1965
Craig, Roger   1962-63
Daviault, Ray   1962
Davis, Tommy   1967
DeMerit, John   1962
Denehy, Bill   1967
DiLauro, Jack   1969
Dillon, Steve   1963-64
Drake, Sammy   1962
Dyer, Don   1968-69
Eilers, Dave   1965-66
Elliot, Larry   1964, 1966
Estrada, Chuck   1967
Fernandez, Chico   1963
Fisher, Jack   1964-67
Fitzmaurice, Shaun   1966
Foss, Larry   1962
Friend, Bob   1966

Frisella, Danny   1967-69
Gardner, Rob   1965-66
Garrett, Wayne   1969
Gaspar, Rod   1969
Gentry, Gary   1969
Ginsberg, Joe   1962
Gonder, Jesse   1963-65
Goossen, Greg   1965-68
Gosger, Jim   1969
Graham, Bill   1967
Graham, Wayne   1964
Green, Dallas   1966
Green, Pumpsie   1963
Grote, Jerry   1966-69
Grzenda, Joe   1967
Hamilton, Jack   1966-67
Harkness, Tim   1963-64
Harrelson, Bud   1965-69
Heise, Bob   1967-69
Hendley, Bob   1967
Hepler, Bill   1966
Herrscher, Rick   1962
Hickman, Jim   1962-66
Hicks, Joe   1963
Hiller, Chuck   1965-67
Hillman, Dave   1962
Hinsley, Jerry   1964, 1967
Hodges, Gil   1962-63
Hook, Jay   1962-64
Hudson, Jesse   1969
Hunt, Ron   1963-66
Hunter, Willard   1962, 1964
Jackson, Al   1962-65, 1968-69
Johnson, Bob D.   1969
Johnson, Bob W.   1967
Jones, Cleon   1963, 1965-69
Jones, Sherman   1962
Jorgensen, Mike   1968
Kanehl, Rod   1962-64
Klaus, Bobby   1964-65
Klimchock, Lou   1966
Kolb, Gary   1965
Koonce, Cal   1967-69
Koosman, Jerry   1967-69
Kranepool, Ed   1962-69
Kroll, Gary   1964-65
Labine, Clem   1962
Lamabe, Jack   1967
Landrith, Hobie   1962
Lary, Frank   1964-65

Lewis, Johnny   1965-67
Linz, Phil   1967-68
Locke, Ron   1964
Luplow, Al   1966-67
McAndrew, Jim   1968-69
McGraw, Frank   1965-67, 1969
MacKenzie, Ken   1962-63
McMillan, Roy   1964-66
Mantilla, Felix   1962
Marshall, Jim   1962
Martin, J. C.   1968-69
Miller, Bob G.   1962
Miller, Bob L.   1962
Miller, Larry   1965-66
Mizell, Wilmer   1962
Moford, Herb   1962
Moock, Joe   1967
Moorhead, Bob   1962, 1965
Moran, Al   1963-64
Murphy, Bill   1966
Musgraves, Dennis   1965
Napoleon, Dan   1965-66
Neal, Charlie   1962-63
Otis, Amos   1967-69
Parsons, Tom   1964-65
Pfeil, Bobby   1969
Piersall, Jim   1963
Pignatano, Joe   1962
Powell, Grover   1963
Reniff, Hal   1967
Reynolds, Tom   1967
Ribant, Dennis   1964-66
Richardson, Gordon   1965-66
Rohr, Les   1967-69
Rowe, Don   1963
Rusteck, Dick   1966
Ryan, Nolan   1966, 1968-69
Samuel, Amado   1964
Schaffer, Jim   1965
Schmelz, Al   1967
Schreiber, Ted   1963
Seaver, Tom   1967-69
Selma, Dick   1965-68
Shamsky, Art   1968-69
Shaw, Bob   1966-67
Shaw, Don   1967-68
Sherry, Norm   1963
Shirley, Bart   1967
Short, Bill   1968
Smith, Bobby Gene   1962
Smith, Charley   1964-65
Smith, Dick   1963-64
Snider, Duke   1963

Spahn, Warren   1965
Stahl, Larry   1967-68
Stallard, Tracy   1963-64
Stephenson, John   1965-66
Stuart, Dick   1966
Sturdivant, Tom   1964
Sullivan, John   1967
Sutherland, Darrell   1964-66
Swoboda, Ron   1965-69
Taylor, Bob "Hank"   1964-67
Taylor, Ron   1967-69
Taylor, Sammy   1962-63
Terry, Ralph   1966-67
Thomas, Frank   1962-64
Throneberry, Marv   1962-63
Wakefield, Bill   1964
Weis, Al   1968-69
Willey, Carl   1963-65
Willhite, Nick   1967
Woodling, Gene   1962
Wynne, Billy   1967
Zimmer, Don   1962

MANAGERS

Hodges, Gil   1968-69
*Parker, Salty   1967
Stengel, Casey   1962-65
Westrum, Wes   1965-67

* Interim manager from September 21 to the end of the season.

COACHES

Berra, Yogi   1965-69
Haddix, Harvey   1966-67
Harder, Mel   1964
Heffner, Don   1964-65
Hemus, Solly   1962-63
Herzog, Whitey   1966
Hornsby, Rogers   1962
Kress, Red   1962
Lavagetto, Cookie   1962-63
McCullough, Clyde   1963
Murphy, John   1967
Parker, Salty   1967
Pignatano, Joe   1968-69
Robinson, Sheriff   1964-67
Ruffing, Red   1962
Spahn, Warren   1965
Walker, Al "Rube"   1968-69
Westrum, Wes   1964-65
White, Ernie   1963
Yost, Ed   1968-69

Met Annual Leaders

1962

BATTING: Avg.—Ashburn, .306; R—Thomas, 69; H—Thomas, 152; 2B—Thomas, 23; 3B—Neal, 9; HR—Thomas, 34; RBI—Thomas, 94; BB—Ashburn, 81; SO—Hickman, 96; SB—Ashburn, Chacon, 12 each; HBP—Thomas, 8.

PITCHING: G—Anderson, 50; ST—Hook, 34; CG—Craig, Hook, 13 each; W—Craig, 10; L—Craig, 24; IP—Craig, 233; H—Craig, 261; R—Hook, 137; ER—Craig, 117; HR—Craig, 35; BB—Jackson, 78; SO—Craig, Jackson, 118 each; ShO—Jackson, 4; ERA—Jackson, 4.40.

1963

BATTING: Avg.—Hunt, .272; R—Hunt, 64; H—Hunt, 145; 2B—Hunt, 28; 3B—Hickman, 6; HR—Hickman, 17; RBI—Thomas, 60; BB—Snider, 56; SO—Hickman, 120; SB—Kanehl, 6; HBP—Hunt, 13.

PITCHING: G—Bearnarth, 58; ST—Jackson, 34; CG—Craig, 14; W—Jackson, 13; L—Craig, 22; IP—Jackson, 227; H—Craig, 249; R—Jackson, 128; ER—Jackson, 100; HR—Craig, 28; BB—Jackson, 84; SO—Jackson, 142; ShO—Willey, 4; ERA—Willey, 3.10.

1964

BATTING: Avg.—Hunt, .303; R—Christopher, 78; H—Christopher, 163; 2B—Christopher, 26; 3B—Christopher, 8; HR—C. Smith, 20; RBI—Christopher, 76; BB—Christopher, 48; SO—C. Smith, 101; SB—Christopher, Hunt, D. Smith, 6 each; HBP—Hunt, 13.

PITCHING: G—Wakefield, 62; ST—Fisher, Stallard, 34 each; CG—Jackson, Stallard, 11 each; W—Jackson, 11; L—Stallard, 20; IP—Fisher, 228; H—Fisher, 256; R—Fisher, 124; ER—Fisher, 107; HR—Fisher, 23; BB—Stallard, 73; SO—Stallard, 118; ShO—Jackson, 3; ERA—Cisco, 3.61.

1965

BATTING: Avg.—Kranepool, .253; R—Lewis, 64; H—Kranepool, 133; 2B—Kranepool, 24; 3B—Kranepool, 4; HR—Swoboda, 19; RBI—C. Smith, 62; BB—Lewis, 59; SO—C. Smith, 123; SB—Christopher, Lewis, 4 each; HBP—Christopher, Hunt, 6 each.

PITCHING: G—Fisher, 43; ST—Fisher, 36; CG—Fisher, 10; W—Fisher, Jackson, 8 each; L—Fisher, 24; IP—Fisher, 254; H—Fisher, 252; R—Fisher, 121; ER—Fisher, 111; HR—Fisher, 22; BB—Fisher, 68; SO—Jackson, 120; ShO—Jackson, 3; ERA—Fisher, 3.93.

1966

BATTING: Avg.—Hunt, .288; R—Jones, 74; H—Hunt, 138; 2B—Boyer, 28; 3B—Bressoud, 5; HR—Kranepool, 16; RBI—Boyer, 61; BB—Bressoud, 47; SO—Bressoud, 107; SB—Jones, 16; HBP—Hunt, 11.

PITCHING: G—Hamilton, 57; ST—Fisher, 33; CG—Fisher, Ribant, 10 each; W—Fisher, Ribant, Shaw, 11 each; L—Fisher, 14; IP—Fisher, 230; H—Fisher, 229; R—Fisher, 108; ER—Fisher, 94; HR—Fisher, 26; BB—Hamilton, 88; SO—Fisher, 127; ShO—Fisher, Shaw, 2 each; ERA—Ribant, 3.21.

1967

BATTING: Avg.—Davis, .302; R—Davis, 72; H—Davis, 174; 2B—Davis, 32; 3B—Jones, 5; HR—Davis, 16; RBI—Davis, 73; BB—Harrelson, 48; SO—Buchek, 101; SB—Harrelson, Jones, 12 each; HBP—Charles, Davis, 7 each.

PITCHING: G—Taylor, 50; ST—Seaver, 34; CG—Seaver, 18; W—Seaver, 16; L—Fisher, 18; IP—Seaver, 251; H—Fisher, 251; R—Fisher, 121; ER—Fisher, 115; HR—Fisher, 21; BB—Seaver, 78; SO—Seaver, 170; ShO—Cardwell, 3; ERA—Seaver, 2.76.

1968

BATTING: Avg.—Jones, .297; R—Jones, 63; H—Jones, 151; 2B—Jones, 29; 3B—Swoboda, 6; HR—Charles, 15; RBI—Swoboda, 59; BB—Swoboda, 52; SO—Swoboda, 113; SB—Jones, 23; HBP—Shamsky, 7.

PITCHING: G—Taylor, 58; ST—Seaver, 35; CG—Koosman, 17; W—Koosman, 19; L—Cardwell, 13; IP—Seaver, 278; H—Seaver, 224; R—Seaver, 73; ER—Seaver, 68; HR—Koosman, 16; BB—Ryan, 75; SO—Seaver, 205; ShO—Koosman, 7; ERA—Koosman, 2.08.

1969

BATTING: Avg.—Jones, .340; R—Agee, 97; H—Jones, 164; 2B—Jones, 25; 3B—Boswell, 7; HR—Agee, 26; RBI—Agee, 76; BB—Jones, 64; SO—Agee, 137; SB—Jones, 16; HBP—Jones, 7.

PITCHING: G—Taylor, 59; ST—Gentry, Seaver, 35 each; CG—Seaver, 18; W—Seaver, 25; L—Gentry, 12; IP—Seaver, 273; H—Gentry, Seaver, 202 each; R—Gentry, 94; ER—Gentry, 89; HR—Gentry, Seaver, 24 each; BB—Seaver, 82; SO—Seaver, 208; ShO—Koosman, 6; ERA—Seaver, 2.21.

All-Time Met Season Records

INDIVIDUAL BATTING

Highest batting average—.340	Cleon Jones	1969
Most games—157	Roy McMillan	1965
Most runs—97	Tommie Agee	1969
Most hits—174	Tommy Davis	1967
Most singles—126	Tommy Davis	1967
Most doubles—32	Tommy Davis	1967
Most triples—9	Charlie Neal	1962
Most home runs, RH—34	Frank Thomas	1962
Most home Runs, LH—16	Marv Throneberry	1962
16	Ed Kranepool	1966
Most home runs, rookie—19	Ron Swoboda	1965
Most home runs, at home—18	Frank Thomas	1962
Most home runs, on road—16	Frank Thomas	1962
Most runs batted in—94	Frank Thomas	1962
Most total bases—283	Frank Thomas	1962
Highest slugging percentage—.496	Frank Thomas	1962
Most stolen bases—23	Cleon Jones	1968
Most walks—81	Richie Ashburn	1962

Most strikeouts—137 .... Tommie Agee 1969
Fewest strikeouts—16 .... Roy McMillan (416 AB) 1964
Most hit by pitcher—13 .... Ron Hunt 1963
Most sacrifice flies—8 .... Ed Kranepool 1965
Most grounded into DP—23 .... Frank Thomas 1963
Fewest grounded into DP—4 .... Richie Ashburn 1962
Consecutive game hit streak—18 .... Frank Thomas 1962
Most pinch hits—14 .... Chuck Hiller 1966

INDIVIDUAL PITCHING

Most games—62 .... Bill Wakefield 1964
Most games started—36 .... Jack Fisher 1965
Most complete games—18 .... Tom Seaver 1967
                18 .... Tom Seaver 1969
Most games won—25 .... Tom Seaver 1969
Most games lost—24 .... Roger Craig 1962
               24 .... Jack Fisher 1965
Most consecutive games won—10 .... Tom Seaver 1969
Most consecutive games lost—18 .... Roger Craig 1963
Most consecutive scoreless innings—23 .... Jim McAndrew 1969
               23 .... Jerry Koosman 1969
Most innings—278 .... Tom Seaver 1968
Most hits—261 .... Roger Craig 1962
Most runs—137 .... Jay Hook 1962
Most earned runs—117 .... Roger Craig 1962
Most walks—88 .... Jack Hamilton 1966
Most strikeouts—208 .... Tom Seaver 1969
Most shutouts—7 .... Jerry Koosman 1968
Most home runs allowed—35 .... Roger Craig 1962
Most hit batsmen—12 .... Al Jackson 1963
Most wild pitches—18 .... Jack Hamilton 1966
Most saves—14 .... Ron Taylor 1968
Lowest earned-run average—2.08 .... Jerry Koosman 1968
   (Minimum 162 innings)

CLUB RECORDS

Most games—164 (1965)
Games won—100 (1969)
Games won, home—52 (1969)
Games won, road—48 (1969)
Games lost—120 (1962)
Games lost, home—58 (1962)
Games lost, road—64 (1963)

Won-lost percentage—.617 (1969)
Most times shut out—30 (1963)
Winning streak—11 (1969)
   (May 28-June 10)
Losing streak—17 (1962)
   (May 21-June 6)

CLUB BATTING

Most runs—632 (1969)
Most hits—1372 (1964)
Most singles—1043 (1964)
Most doubles—203 (1965)
Most triples—41 (1969)
Most home runs—139 (1962)

Most grand-slam home runs—4 (1963)
Most runs batted in—598 (1969)
Most stolen bases—72 (1968)
Most walks—616 (1962)
Most strikeouts—1203 (1968)
Batting percentage—.246 (1964)

CLUB PITCHING

Most complete games—51 (1969)

Most runs allowed—948 (1962)

Fewest runs allowed—499 (1968)

Most walks—571 (1962)

Fewest walks—430 (1968)

Most strikeouts—1014 (1968)

Fewest strikeouts—717 (1964)

Most home runs allowed—192 (1962)

Fewest home runs allowed—87 (1968)

Highest earned-run avg.—5.04 (1962)

Lowest earned-run avg.—2.72 (1968)

Most shutouts—28 (1969)

One-Game Records

INDIVIDUAL PITCHING

Strikeouts (9 innings)—14: Nolan Ryan vs. Cincinnati, May 14, 1968, and Tom Seaver vs. San Diego, June 8, 1969.

Strikeouts (extra inning)—15: Jerry Koosman vs. San Diego, May 28, 1969 (10 innings).

Walks—7: Last time by Don Cardwell vs. San Francisco, August 30, 1969.

Innings pitched—15: Al Jackson vs. Philadelphia, August 14, 1962, and Rob Gardner vs. Philadelphia, October 2, 1965.

INDIVIDUAL BATTING

Hits—5: Dick Smith vs. Chicago, May 26, 1964; Jim Hickman vs. Milwaukee, September 30, 1964; and Phil Linz vs. Philadelphia, July 6, 1968.

Runs—4: Last time by Tommie Agee vs. Montreal, July 13, 1969.

Doubles—3: Dick Smith vs. Milwaukee, May 14, 1964; Ron Hunt vs. San Francisco, August 27, 1965; Ken Boyer vs. Atlanta, April 17, 1966; and Kevin Collins vs. San Francisco, June 15, 1968.

Triples—2: Last time by Bud Harrelson vs. San Francisco, September 16, 1966.

Home runs—3: Jim Hickman vs. St. Louis, September 3, 1965.

Runs batted in—6: Frank Thomas vs. Philadelphia, August 1, 1962, and Jerry Buchek vs. Houston, September 22, 1967.

Total bases—13: Jim Hickman (3 homers, 1 single) vs. St. Louis, September 3, 1965.

Stolen bases—3: Tim Harkness vs. Philadelphia, September 9, 1963.

Sacrifice flies—2: Jesse Gonder vs. Milwaukee, August 3, 1963, and Cleon Jones vs. San Francisco, July 26, 1967.

Sacrifice bunts—2: Last time by Bob Pfeil vs. San Diego, August 26, 1969.

TEAM

Hits—23: May 26, 1964, vs. Chicago.

Runs—19: May 26, 1964, vs. Chicago.

Runs, inning—8: June 26, 1964, vs. Milwaukee (2nd inning) and May 14, 1969, vs. Atlanta (8th inning).

Home runs—5: April 28, 1962, vs. Philadelphia—Charlie Neal (2), Jim Hickman, Gil Hodges, Frank Thomas. August 3, 1962, vs. Cincinnati—Frank Thomas (2), Clarence Coleman, Charlie Neal, Marv Throneberry. October 3, 1964, vs. St. Louis —George Altman, Joe Christopher, Bobby Klaus, Ed Kranepool, Charley Smith.

Hits allowed—22: June 16, 1966, vs. Atlanta.

Runs allowed—17: Last time: June 16, 1966, vs. Atlanta.

Left on bases (9 innings)—15: September 11, 1963, vs. San Francisco and May 11, 1969, vs. Houston (2nd game).

Left on bases (extra innings)—19: May 15, 1962, vs. Chicago.
Players used (9 innings)—21: September 16, 1966, vs. San Francisco.
Players used (extra innings)—22: April 15, 1968, vs. Houston.
Pitchers used (9 innings)—7: July 10, 1966, vs. Pittsburgh.
Pitchers used (extra innings)—8: April 15, 1968, vs. Houston.
Longest game, innings—24: April 15, 1968, vs. Houston.
Longest game, time (9 innings)—3:50: August 8, 1965, vs. Chicago.
Longest game, time (extra innings)—7:23: May 31, 1964, vs. San Francisco.
Shortest game, time—1:39: July 27, 1963, vs. Houston.

Met Opening-Day Lineups

1962	**1963**	**1964**	**1965**
Ashburn, cf	Burright, 2b	D. Smith, 1b	Cowan, cf
Mantilla, ss	Coleman, c	Samuel, 2b	McMillan, ss
Neal, 2b	Kranepool, rf	Hunt, 3b	Lewis, rf
Thomas, lf	Snider, cf	Thomas, lf	Kranepool, 1b
Bell, rf	Thomas, lf	Hickman, cf	Christopher, lf
Hodges, 1b	Harkness, 1b	B. Taylor, c	C. Smith, 3b
Zimmer, 3b	Neal, 3b	Christopher, rf	Klaus, 2b
Landrith, c	Moran, ss	Moran, ss	Cannizzaro, c
Craig, p	Craig, p	Jackson, p	Jackson, p

1966	**1967**	**1968**	**1969**
Jones, rf	Bosch, cf	Harrelson, ss	Agee, cf
Hunt, 2b	Jones, rf	Boswell, 2b	Gaspar, rf
Boyer, 3b	Boyer, 3b	Agee, cf	Boswell, 2b
Stuart, 1b	Davis, lf	Swoboda, rf	Jones, lf
Hickman, cf	Swoboda, 1b	Kranepool, 1b	Charles, 3b
Swoboda, lf	Buchek, 2b	Shamsky, lf	Kranepool, 1b
Grote, c	Grote, c	Martin, c	Grote, c
McMillan, ss	Harrelson, ss	Charles, 3b	Harrelson, ss
Fisher, p	Cardwell, p	Seaver, p	Seaver, p

Met Opening-Day Results

APRIL 11, 1962, AT ST. LOUIS:

Mets	0 0 2 1 1 0 0 0 0 —	4	8	2
St. Louis	2 0 3 0 1 4 0 1 x —	11	16	1

Mets: Craig, Moorhead (4), Moford (7), Labine (8), and Landrith.
StL: L. Jackson and Oliver.
W.P.—Jackson. L.P.—Craig. HR—Mets: Hodges and Neal.

APRIL 9, 1963, VS. ST. LOUIS AT POLO GROUNDS:

St. Louis	2 0 2 0 0 3 0 0 0 —	7	14	0
Mets	0 0 0 0 0 0 0 0 0 —	0	2	2

StL: Broglio and Sawatski.
Mets: Craig, Rowe (6), Cisco (9), and Coleman.
W.P.—Broglio. L.P.—Craig. HR—StL: White.

APRIL 14, 1964, AT PHILADELPHIA:

Mets	000	120	000—	3	11	1
Philadelphia	310	000	01 x—	5	6	0

Mets: Jackson, Bearnarth (8), and B. Taylor.
Phila: Bennett, Klippstein (5), and Dalrymple.
W.P.—Klippstein. L.P.—Jackson. HR—Mets: Christopher; Phila: Sievers.

APRIL 12, 1965, VS. LOS ANGELES AT SHEA:

Los Angeles	201	210	000—	6	8	0
Mets	000	100	000—	1	4	0

LA: Drysdale and Roseboro.
Mets: Jackson, Lary (6), Parsons (7), Bethke (9), and Cannizzaro, Gonder.
W.P.—Drysdale. L.P.—Jackson. HR—LA: W. Davis and Drysdale.

APRIL 15, 1966, VS. ATLANTA AT SHEA:

Atlanta	000	001	002—	3	7	2
Mets	100	000	010—	2	6	1

Atl: Lemaster, O'Dell (9), and Torre.
Mets: Fisher and Grote.
W.P.—Lemaster. L.P.—Fisher. HR—Mets: Jones.

APRIL 11, 1967, VS. PITTSBURGH AT SHEA:

Pittsburgh	001	002	003—	6	8	1
Mets	100	200	000—	3	5	5

Pitt: Veale, Mikkelsen (9), and Gonder, May.
Mets: Cardwell, D. Shaw (9), and Grote.
W.P.—Veale. L.P.—Cardwell. HR—Mets: Grote.

APRIL 10, 1968, AT SAN FRANCISCO:

Mets	103	000	000—	4	9	2
San Francisco	001	000	103—	5	9	0

Mets: Seaver, Frisella (9), and Martin, Grote.
SF: Marichal, Linzy (9), and Hiatt, Barton.
W.P.—Linzy. L.P.—Frisella. HR—Mets: Swoboda; SF: McCovey.

APRIL 8, 1969, VS. MONTREAL AT SHEA:

Montreal	201	102	140—11	12	0
Mets	030	300	004—10	15	3

Mont.: Grant, McGinn (2), Robertson (4), Shaw (6), Sembera (9), and Bateman.
Mets: Seaver, Koonce (6), Jackson (8), Taylor (8), and Grote.
W.P.—Shaw. L.P.—Koonce. HR—Mets: Dyer; Mont.: McGinn, Staub, and Laboy.

The 22 Original Expansion Mets

The 22 original Mets selected in the expansion draft of October 10, 1961:

$125,000

Pitchers—Jay Hook (Cincinnati) and Bob L. Miller (St. Louis); infielder—Don Zimmer (Chicago); Outfielder—Lee Walls (Philadelphia).

$75,000

Pitchers—Craig Anderson (St. Louis), Roger Craig (Los Angeles), Ray Daviault (San Francisco), and Al Jackson (Pittsburgh); Catchers—Chris Cannizzaro (St. Louis), Clarence Coleman (Philadelphia), and Hobie Landrith (San Francisco); Infielders— Ed Bouchee (Chicago), Elio Chacon (Cincinnati), Sammy Drake (Chicago), Gil Hodges (Los Angeles), and Felix Mantilla (Milwaukee); Outfielders—Gus Bell (Cincinnati), Joe Christopher (Pittsburgh), John DeMerit (Milwaukee), and Bobby Gene Smith (Philadelphia).

$50,000

Pitcher—Sherman Jones (Cincinnati); Outfielder—Jim Hickman (St. Louis).

Year-by-Year Record

YEAR	W	L	PCT.	POS	GB	MANAGER
1962	40	120	.250	10	60½	Stengel
1963	51	111	.315	10	48	Stengel
1964	53	109	.327	10	40	Stengel
1965	50	112	.309	10	47	Stengel-Westrum
1966	66	95	.410	9	28½	Westrum
1967	61	101	.377	10	40½	Westrum-Parker
1968	73	89	.451	9	24	Hodges
*1969	100	62	.617	1	—	Hodges

* World Champions.

All-Star Game Selections

1962—Richie Ashburn
1963—Duke Snider
1964—Ron Hunt*
1968—Jerry Grote,* Jerry Koosman, and Tom Seaver
1969—Cleon Jones,* Jerry Koosman, and Tom Seaver

1965—Ed Kranepool
1966—Ron Hunt
1967—Tom Seaver

* Starter selected by players.

1969 Met Statistics

BATTING

	G	AB	R	H	2B	3B	HR	RBI	BB	SO	SB-C	DP	SH	SF	HB	E	AVG
Agee	149	565	97	153	23	4	26	76	59	137	12-8	6	6	2	3	5	.271
Boswell	102	362	48	101	14	7	3	32	36	47	7-3	13	4	1	2	18	.279
Charles	61	169	21	35	8	1	3	18	18	31	4-2	6	0	1	1	7	.207
Clendenon*	72	202	31	51	5	0	12	37	19	62	3-2	3	2	1	2	7	.252
Collins	16	40	1	6	3	0	1	2	3	10	0-0	0	0	0	0	3	.150
Dyer	29	74	5	19	3	1	3	12	4	22	0-0	3	1	0	0	1	.257
Garrett	124	400	38	87	11	3	1	39	40	75	4-2	5	6	5	3	11	.218
Gaspar	118	215	26	49	6	1	1	14	25	19	7-3	1	7	1	2	2	.228
Gosger	10	15	0	2	2	0	0	1	1	6	0-0	0	0	0	0	0	.133
Grote	113	365	38	92	12	3	6	40	32	59	2-1	11	6	2	1	7	.252
Harrelson	123	395	42	98	11	6	0	24	54	54	1-3	5	5	1	2	19	.248

	G	AB	R	H	2B	3B	HR	RBI	BB	SO	SB-C	DP	SH	SF	HB	E	AVG
Heise	4	10	1	3	1	0	0	0	3	2	0-0	1	0	0	0	0	.300
Jones	137	483	92	164	25	4	12	75	64	60	16-7	10	1	3	7	2	.340
Kranepool	112	353	36	84	9	2	11	49	37	32	3-2	10	2	4	0	6	.238
Martin	66	177	12	37	5	1	4	21	12	32	0-0	6	1	2	0	1	.209
Otis	47	93	6	14	3	1	0	4	6	27	1-0	0	3	0	0	1	.151
Pfeil	62	211	20	49	9	0	0	10	7	27	0-0	5	4	0	1	4	.232
Shamsky	100	303	42	91	9	3	14	47	36	32	1-2	6	2	4	2	2	.300
Swoboda	109	327	38	77	10	2	9	52	43	90	1-1	10	1	2	2	2	.235
Weis	103	247	20	53	9	2	2	23	15	51	3-3	3	6	1	0	13	.215
Cardwell	30	47	3	8	0	0	1	5	0	25	0-0	0	2	1	1	3	.170
DiLauro	23	12	0	0	0	0	0	0	0	9	0-0	0	0	0	0	0	.000
Frisella	3	1	0	0	0	0	0	0	0	0	0-0	0	0	0	0	0	.000
Gentry	35	74	2	6	1	0	0	1	1	49	0-0	0	7	1	1	0	.081
Hudson	1	0	0	0	0	0	0	0	0	0	0-0	0	0	0	0	0	.000
Jackson	9	1	0	0	0	0	0	0	0	0	0-0	0	0	0	0	0	.000
Johnson	2	0	0	0	0	0	0	0	0	0	0-0	0	0	0	0	0	.000
Koonce	40	17	1	4	0	0	0	1	0	7	0-0	0	0	0	0	0	.235
Koosman	32	84	1	4	0	0	0	1	1	47	0-0	2	4	0	0	1	.048
McAndrew	27	37	0	5	1	0	0	3	3	18	0-1	0	5	0	0	0	.135
McGraw	43	24	1	4	1	0	0	3	1	5	0-0	0	0	0	0	2	.167
Rohr	1	0	0	0	0	0	0	0	0	0	0-0	0	0	0	0	0	.000
Ryan	26	29	3	3	0	0	0	2	0	15	0-0	0	3	0	0	1	.103
Seaver	39	91	7	11	3	0	0	6	6	34	1-0	0	4	0	2	2	.121
Taylor	59	4	0	1	0	0	0	0	0	2	0-0	0	0	0	0	0	.250
TOTAL	162	5427	632	1311	184	41	109	598	527	1088	66-40	103	82	33	33	119	.242

* Does not include totals with Montreal.

PITCHING

	G	ST	CG	W-L	IP	H	R	ER	BB	SO	HR	SHO	Saves	ERA
Cardwell	30	21	4	8-10	152⅓	145	63	51	47	60	15	0	0	3.02
DiLauro	23	4	0	1-4	63⅔	50	19	17	18	27	4	0	1	2.39
Frisella	3	0	0	0-0	4⅔	8	4	4	3	5	1	0	0	7.20
Gentry	35	35	6	13-12	233⅔	202	94	89	81	154	24	3	0	3.42
Hudson	1	0	0	0-0	2	2	1	1	2	3	0	0	0	4.50
Jackson	9	0	0	0-0	11	18	13	13	4	10	1	0	0	10.64
Johnson	2	0	0	0-0	1⅔	1	0	0	1	1	0	0	1	0.00
Koonce	40	0	0	6-3	83	85	53	46	42	48	8	0	7	4.99
Koosman	32	32	16	17-9	241	187	66	61	68	180	14	6	0	2.28
McAndrew	27	21	4	6-7	135	112	57	52	44	90	12	2	0	3.47
McGraw	42	4	1	9-3	100⅓	89	31	25	47	92	6	0	12	2.25
Rohr	1	0	0	0-0	1⅓	5	4	3	1	0	0	0	0	27.00
Ryan	25	10	2	6-3	89⅓	60	38	35	53	92	3	0	1	3.54
Seaver	36	35	18	25-7	273⅓	202	75	67	82	208	24	5	0	2.21
Taylor	59	0	0	9-4	76	61	23	23	24	42	7	0	13	2.72
TOTAL	162	162	51	100-62	1468⅓	1217	541	487	517	1012	119	*28	35	2.99

* Twelve combined shutouts.

1969 Playoff Results

FIRST GAME

Mets	0 2 0	2 0 0	0 5 0 —	9	10	1
Atlanta	0 1 2	0 1 0	1 0 0 —	5	10	2

Mets: Seaver, Taylor (8), and Grote.
Atl: Niekro, Upshaw (9), and Didier.
W.P.: Seaver. **L.P.:** Niekro. **HR**—Atl: Gonzalez and H. Aaron.

SECOND GAME

| Mets | 1 3 2 | 2 1 0 | 2 0 0 — 11 | 13 | 1 |
| Atlanta | 0 0 0 | 1 5 0 | 0 0 0 — 6 | 9 | 3 |

Mets: Koosman, Taylor (5), McGraw (7), and Grote.
Atl: Reed, Doyle (2), Pappas (3), Britton (6), Upshaw (6), Neibauer (9), and Didier.
W.P.: Taylor. L.P.: Reed. HR—Mets: Agee, Boswell, and Jones; Atl: H. Aaron.

THIRD GAME

| Atlanta | 2 0 0 | 0 2 0 | 0 0 0 — 4 | 8 | 1 |
| Mets | 0 0 1 | 2 3 1 | 0 0 x — 7 | 14 | 0 |

Atl: Jarvis, Stone (5), Upshaw (6), and Didier, Tillman.
Mets: Gentry, Ryan (3), and Grote.
W.P.: Ryan. L.P.: Jarvis. HR—Atl: H. Aaron and Cepeda; Mets: Agee, Boswell, and Garrett.

1969 Playoff Averages

BATTING

	G	AB	R	H	2B	3B	HR	RBI	BB	SO	SB-C	SH	SF	AVG
Shamsky	3	13	3	7	0	0	0	1	0	3	0-0	0	0	.538
Ryan	1	4	1	2	0	0	0	0	0	1	0-0	0	0	.500
Martin	2	2	0	1	0	0	0	2	0	0	0-0	0	0	.500
Jones	3	14	4	6	2	0	1	4	1	2	2-0	0	0	.429
Garrett	3	13	3	5	2	0	1	3	2	2	1-0	0	0	.385
Agee	3	14	4	5	1	0	2	4	2	5	2-0	0	0	.357
Boswell	3	12	4	4	0	0	2	5	1	2	0-0	0	0	.333
Kranepool	3	12	2	3	1	0	0	1	1	2	0-1	0	0	.250
Harrelson	3	11	2	2	1	1	0	3	1	2	0-0	1	0	.182
Grote	3	12	3	2	1	0	0	1	1	4	0-0	0	0	.167
Weis	3	1	0	0	0	0	0	0	0	0	0-0	0	0	.000
Koosman	1	2	1	0	0	0	0	0	1	2	0-0	0	0	.000
Seaver	1	3	0	0	0	0	0	0	0	0	0-0	0	0	.000
Gentry	1	0	0	0	0	0	0	0	0	0	0-0	0	0	.000
McGraw	1	0	0	0	0	0	0	0	0	0	0-0	0	0	.000
Taylor	2	0	0	0	0	0	0	0	0	0	0-0	0	0	.000
Gaspar	3	0	0	0	0	0	0	0	0	0	0-0	0	0	.000
TOTAL	3	113	27	37	8	1	6	24	10	25	5-1	1	0	.327

PITCHING

	G	ST	CG	W-L	IP	H	R	ER	BB	SO	HR	Saves	ERA
Taylor	2	0	0	1-0	3⅓	3	0	0	0	4	0	1	0.00
McGraw	1	0	0	0-0	3	1	0	0	1	1	0	1	0.00
Ryan	1	0	0	1-0	7	3	2	2	2	7	1	0	2.57
Seaver	1	1	0	1-0	7	8	5	5	3	2	2	0	6.43
Gentry	1	1	0	0-0	2	5	2	2	1	1	1	0	9.00
Koosman	1	1	0	0-0	4⅔	7	6	6	4	5	1	0	10.80
TOTAL	3	3	0	3-0	27	27	15	15	11	20	5	2	5.00

World Series

FIRST GAME

METS

	AB	R	H	2B	3B	HR	TB	BB	SO	RBI	PO	A	E
Agee, cf	4	0	0	0	0	0	0	0	2	0	4	0	0
Harrelson, ss	3	0	1	0	0	0	1	1	0	0	0	1	0
Jones, lf	4	0	1	0	0	0	1	0	0	0	1	0	0
Clendenon, 1b	4	1	2	1	0	0	3	0	2	0	9	1	0
Swoboda, rf	3	0	1	0	0	0	1	1	1	0	0	0	0
Charles, 3b	4	0	0	0	0	0	0	0	1	0	1	4	0
Grote, c	4	0	1	0	0	0	1	0	1	0	6	0	0
Weis, 2b	1	0	0	0	0	0	0	2	0	1	3	1	1
Seaver, p	1	0	0	0	0	0	0	0	1	0	0	0	0
Dyer*	1	0	0	0	0	0	0	0	0	0	0	0	0
Cardwell, p	1	0	0	0	0	0	0	0	0	0	0	0	0
Gaspar†	1	0	0	0	0	0	0	0	0	0	0	0	0
Taylor, p	0	0	0	0	0	0	0	0	0	0	0	0	0
Shamsky‡	0	0	0	0	0	0	0	0	0	0	0	1	0
TOTAL	31	1	6	1	0	0	7	4	8	1	24	8	1

* Grounded out for Seaver in 6th.
† Grounded out for Cardwell in 7th.
‡ Grounded out for Taylor in 9th.

ORIOLES

	AB	R	H	2B	3B	HR	TB	BB	SO	RBI	PO	A	E
Buford, lf	4	1	2	1	0	1	6	0	0	2	2	0	0
Blair, cf	3	0	0	0	0	0	0	1	1	0	2	0	0
F. Robinson, rf	4	0	0	0	0	0	0	0	2	0	2	0	0
Powell, 1b	4	0	1	0	0	0	1	0	0	0	11	0	0
B. Robinson, 3b	4	0	0	0	0	0	0	0	1	0	0	6	0
Hendricks, c	3	1	1	0	0	0	1	0	0	0	8	0	0
Johnson, 2b	2	1	0	0	0	0	0	1	0	0	1	3	0
Belanger, ss	3	1	1	0	0	0	1	0	1	1	1	3	0
Cuellar, p	3	0	1	0	0	0	1	0	2	1	0	0	0
TOTAL	30	4	6	1	0	1	10	2	6	4	27	12	0

Mets	0 0 0	0 0 0	1 0 0—1
Orioles	1 0 0	3 0 0	0 0 0—4

Earned runs—All. Left on bases—Mets 8, Orioles 4. Sacrifice fly—Weis. Double play—Baltimore 1 (Belanger-Johnson-Powell). Bases on balls—off Seaver 1 (Johnson); Taylor 1 (Blair); Cuellar 4 (Weis 2, Harrelson, Swoboda). Struck out—by Seaver 3 (Blair, F. Robinson, Cuellar); Taylor 3 (Cuellar, F. Robinson, B. Robinson); Cuellar 8 (Clendenon 2, Swoboda, Charles, Seaver, Agee 2, Grote). Hits—off Seaver 6 and 4 runs (4 earned) in 5 inns.; Cardwell 0 and 0 (0) in 1; Taylor 0 and 0 (0) in 2. Picked off—by Taylor 1 (Blair). Winning pitcher—Cuellar. Losing pitcher—Seaver. Time 2:13. Umpires—Soar (AL), Secory (NL), Napp (AL), Crawford (NL), DiMuro (AL), Weyer (NL). Attendance—50,429.

SECOND GAME

METS

	AB	R	H	2B	3B	HR	TB	BB	SO	RBI	PO	A	E
Agee, cf	4	0	0	0	0	0	0	0	2	0	3	0	0
Harrelson, ss	3	0	0	0	0	0	0	1	0	0	3	3	0
Jones, lf	4	0	0	0	0	0	0	0	0	0	2	0	0
Clendenon, 1b	3	1	1	0	0	1	4	1	1	1	7	0	0
Swoboda, rf	4	0	0	0	0	0	0	0	1	0	5	0	0
Charles, 3b	4	1	2	1	0	0	3	0	0	0	0	3	0
Grote, c	4	0	1	0	0	0	1	0	0	0	4	0	0
Weis, 2b	3	0	2	0	0	0	2	1	1	1	3	1	0
Koosman, p	4	0	0	0	0	0	0	0	2	0	1	1	0
Taylor, p	0	0	0	0	0	0	0	0	0	0	0	0	0
TOTAL	33	2	6	1	0	1	10	3	7	2	27	8	0

ORIOLES

	AB	R	H	2B	3B	HR	TB	BB	SO	RBI	PO	A	E
Buford, lf	4	0	0	0	0	0	0	0	1	0	1	0	0
Blair, cf	4	1	1	0	0	0	1	0	0	0	2	0	0
F. Robinson, rf	3	0	0	0	0	0	0	1	0	0	2	0	0
Rettenmund*	0	0	0	0	0	0	0	0	0	0	0	0	0
Powell, 1b	3	0	0	0	0	0	0	1	1	0	10	1	0
B. Robinson, 3b	4	0	1	0	0	0	1	0	0	1	0	2	0
Johnson, 2b	2	0	0	0	0	0	0	1	0	0	1	3	0
Etchebarren, c	3	0	0	0	0	0	0	0	0	0	8	0	0
Belanger, ss	3	0	0	0	0	0	0	0	1	0	2	4	0
McNally	3	0	0	0	0	0	0	0	1	0	1	1	0
TOTAL	29	1	2	0	0	0	2	3	4	1	27	11	0

* Ran for F. Robinson in 9th.

Mets	0 0 0	1 0 0	0 0 1—2
Orioles	0 0 0	0 0 0	1 0 0—1

Earned runs—All. Left on bases—Mets 7; Orioles 4. Stolen base—Blair. Bases on balls—off Koosman 3 (Johnson, F. Robinson, Powell); McNally 3 (Clendenon, Harrelson, Weis). Struck out—by Koosman 4 (Buford, Powell, McNally, Belanger); McNally 7 (Agee 2, Koosman 2, Swoboda, Weis, Clendenon). Hits—off Koosman 2 and 1 run (1 earned) in 8⅔ inns.; Taylor 0 and 0 (0) in ⅓. Wild pitch—McNally. Winning Pitcher—Koosman. Losing Pitcher—McNally. Time—2:20. Umpires—Secory (NL), Napp (AL), Crawford (NL), DiMuro (AL), Weyer (NL), Soar (AL). Attendance—50,850.

THIRD GAME

ORIOLES

	AB	R	H	2B	3B	HR	TB	BB	SO	RBI	PO	A	E
Buford, lf	3	0	0	0	0	0	0	2	2	0	2	0	0
Blair, cf	5	0	0	0	0	0	0	0	2	0	0	0	0
F. Robinson, rf	2	0	1	0	0	0	1	2	0	0	7	0	0
Powell, 1b	4	0	2	0	0	0	2	0	1	0	5	1	0
B. Robinson, 3b	4	0	0	0	0	0	0	0	2	0	0	1	0
Hendricks, c	4	0	0	0	0	0	0	0	0	0	6	0	0
Johnson, 2b	4	0	0	0	0	0	0	0	0	0	1	3	0
Belanger, ss	2	0	0	0	0	0	0	2	0	0	2	0	0
Palmer, p	2	0	0	0	0	0	0	0	0	0	1	0	1
May*	0	0	0	0	0	0	0	1	0	0	0	0	0
Leonhard, p	0	0	0	0	0	0	0	0	0	0	0	1	0
Dalrymple†	1	0	1	0	0	0	1	0	0	0	0	0	0
Salmon‡	0	0	0	0	0	0	0	0	0	0	0	0	0
TOTAL	31	0	4	0	0	0	4	7	7	0	24	6	1

* Walked for Palmer in 7th.
† Singled for Leonhard in 9th.
‡ Ran for Dalrymple in 9th.

METS

	AB	R	H	2B	3B	HR	TB	BB	SO	RBI	PO	A	E
Agee, cf	3	1	1	0	0	1	4	1	0	1	6	0	0
Garrett, 3b	1	0	0	0	0	0	0	2	1	0	1	0	0
Jones, lf	4	0	0	0	0	0	0	0	1	0	0	0	0
Shamsky, rf	4	0	0	0	0	0	0	0	0	0	1	0	0
Weis, 2b	0	0	0	0	0	0	0	0	0	0	0	0	0
Boswell, 2b	3	1	1	0	0	0	1	0	0	0	0	1	0
Gaspar, rf	1	0	0	0	0	0	0	0	0	0	2	0	0
Kranepool, 1b	4	1	1	0	0	1	4	0	1	1	6	0	0
Grote, c	3	1	1	1	0	0	2	1	0	1	8	0	0
Harrelson, ss	3	1	1	0	0	0	1	1	2	0	3	5	0
Gentry, p	3	0	1	1	0	0	2	0	2	2	0	0	0
Ryan, p	0	0	0	0	0	0	0	0	0	0	0	0	0
TOTAL	29	5	6	2	0	2	14	5	6	5	27	6	0

Orioles	0 0 0	0 0 0	0 0 0—0
Mets	1 2 0	0 0 1	0 1 x—5

Earned runs—All. Left on bases—Baltimore 11, Mets 5. Sacrifice—Garrett. Bases on balls—off Palmer 4 (Grote, Garrett 2, Harrelson); Leonhard 1 (Agee); Gentry 5 (F. Robinson 2, Belanger, May, Buford); Ryan 2 (Belanger, Buford). Struck out—by Palmer 5 (Garrett, Jones, Gentry 2, Harrelson; Leonhard 1 (Harrelson); Gentry 4 (Buford 2, Blair, B. Robinson); Ryan 3 (Powell, B. Robinson, Blair). Hits—off Palmer 5 and 4 runs (4 earned) in 6 inns; Leonhard 1 and 1 (1) in 2. Gentry 3 and 0 (0) in 6⅔; Ryan 1 and 0 (0) in 2⅓. Winning Pitcher—Gentry. Losing Pitcher—Palmer. Time —2:23. Umpires—Napp (AL), Crawford (NL), DiMuro (AL), Weyer (NL), Soar (AL), Secory (NL). Attendance—56,335.

FOURTH GAME

ORIOLES

	AB	R	H	2B	3B	HR	TB	BB	SO	RBI	PO	A	E
Buford, lf	5	0	0	0	0	0	0	0	1	0	2	0	0
Blair, cf	4	0	1	0	0	0	1	1	1	0	0	0	0
F. Robinson, rf	4	1	1	0	0	0	1	0	0	0	0	0	0
Powell, 1b	4	0	1	0	0	0	1	0	1	0	14	0	0
B. Robinson, 3b	3	0	0	0	0	0	0	0	0	1	0	3	0
Hendricks, c	3	0	0	0	0	0	0	1	0	0	7	1	0
Johnson, 2b	4	0	0	0	0	0	0	0	1	0	4	6	0
Belanger, ss	4	0	1	0	0	0	1	0	0	0	0	6	0
Cuellar, p	2	0	1	0	0	0	1	0	1	0	0	1	0
May*	1	0	0	0	0	0	0	0	1	0	0	0	0
Watt, p	0	0	0	0	0	0	0	0	0	0	0	0	0
Dalrymple†	1	0	1	0	0	0	1	0	0	0	0	0	0
Hall, p	0	0	0	0	0	0	0	0	0	0	0	0	0
Richert, p	0	0	0	0	0	0	0	0	0	0	0	0	1
TOTAL	35	1	6	0	0	0	6	2	6	1	27‡	17	1

* Fanned for Cuellar in 8th.
† Singled for Watt in 10th.
‡ None out when winning run scored.

METS

	AB	R	H	2B	3B	HR	TB	BB	SO	RBI	PO	A	E
Agee, cf	4	0	1	0	0	0	1	0	1	0	2	0	0
Harrelson, ss	4	0	1	0	0	0	1	0	0	0	5	2	0
Jones, lf	4	0	1	0	0	0	1	0	0	0	1	0	0
Clendenon, 1b	4	1	1	0	0	1	4	0	2	1	6	3	0
Swoboda, rf	4	0	3	0	0	0	3	0	0	0	4	0	0
Charles, 3b	3	0	0	0	0	0	0	0	1	0	2	1	0
Shamsky*	1	0	0	0	0	0	0	0	0	0	0	0	0
Garrett, 3b	0	0	0	0	0	0	0	0	0	0	0	0	1
Grote, c	4	0	1	1	0	0	2	0	2	0	7	2	0
Gaspar†	0	1	0	0	0	0	0	0	0	0	0	0	0
Weis, 2b	3	0	2	0	0	0	2	1	0	0	1	1	0
Seaver, p	3	0	0	0	0	0	0	0	1	0	2	1	0
Martin‡	0	0	0	0	0	0	0	0	0	0	0	0	0
TOTAL	34	2	10	1	0	1	14	1	7	1	30	10	1

* Grounded out for Charles in 9th.
† Ran for Grote in 10th.
‡ Sacrificed for Seaver in 10th.

Orioles	0 0 0　　0 0 0　　0 0 1　　0—1
Mets	0 1 0　　0 0 0　　0 0 0　　1—2

Earned runs—Orioles 1, Mets 1. Left on bases—Orioles 7, Mets 7. Caught stealing—by Grote (Johnson); Hendricks (Swoboda). Sacrifice—Martin. Sacrifice Fly—B. Robinson. Double plays—Orioles 3 (Belanger-Johnson-Powell 2; Hendricks-Johnson). Bases on balls—off Hall 1 (Weis); Seaver 2 (Hendricks, Blair). Struck out—by Cuellar 5 (Grote 2, Clendenon, Charles); Watt 2 (Agee, Clendenon); Seaver 6 (Buford, Powell, Cuellar, Johnson, May, Blair). Hits—off Cuellar 7 and 1 run (1 earned) in 7 inns.; Watt 2 and 0 (0) in 2; Hall 1 and 1 (0) in 0 (faced 2 in 10th); Richert 0 and 0 (0) in 0 (faced 1 in 10th). Winning Pitcher—Seaver. Losing Pitcher—Hall. Time—2:33. Umpires—Crawford (NL), DiMuro (AL), Weyer (NL), Soar (AL), Secory (NL), Napp (AL). Attendance—57,367.

FIFTH GAME

ORIOLES

	AB	R	H	2B	3B	HR	TB	BB	SO	RBI	PO	A	E
Buford, lf	4	0	0	0	0	0	0	0	0	0	1	0	0
Blair, cf	4	0	0	0	0	0	0	0	1	0	3	0	0
F. Robinson, rf	3	1	1	0	0	1	4	1	1	1	2	0	0
Powell, 1b	4	0	1	0	0	0	1	0	1	0	6	0	1
Salmon*	0	0	0	0	0	0	0	0	0	0	0	0	0
B. Robinson, 3b	4	0	0	0	0	0	0	0	0	0	1	4	0
Johnson, 2b	4	0	1	0	0	0	1	0	0	0	1	0	0
Etchebarren, c	3	0	0	0	0	0	0	0	1	0	8	0	0
Belanger, ss	3	1	1	0	0	0	1	0	0	0	2	1	0
McNally, p	2	1	1	0	0	1	4	0	1	2	0	0	0
Motton†	1	0	0	0	0	0	0	0	0	0	0	0	0
Watt, p	0	0	0	0	0	0	0	0	0	0	0	0	1
TOTAL	32	3	5	0	0	2	11	1	5	3	24	5	2

METS

	AB	R	H	2B	3B	HR	TB	BB	SO	RBI	PO	A	E
Agee, cf	3	0	1	0	0	0	1	1	0	0	4	0	0
Harrelson, ss	4	0	0	0	0	0	0	0	2	0	1	6	0
Jones, lf	3	2	1	1	0	0	2	0	0	0	3	0	0
Clendenon, 1b	3	1	1	0	0	1	4	1	1	2	8	0	0
Swoboda, rf	4	1	2	1	0	0	3	0	1	1	5	0	0
Charles, 3b	4	0	0	0	0	0	0	0	0	0	0	1	0
Grote, c	4	0	0	0	0	0	0	0	0	0	5	0	0
Weis, 2b	4	1	1	0	0	1	4	0	1	1	1	2	0
Koosman, p	3	0	1	1	0	0	2	0	2	0	0	1	0
TOTAL	32	5	7	3	0	2	16	2	7	4	27	10	0

* Ran for Powell in 9th.
† Grounded out for McNally in 8th.

Orioles	0	0 3		0 0 0		0 0 0—3			
Mets	0	0 0		0 0 2		1 2 x—5			

Earned runs—Orioles 3, Mets 4. Left on bases—Orioles 3, Mets 6. Stolen base—Agee. Bases on balls—off McNally 2 (Agee, Clendenon); Koosman 1 (F. Robinson). Struck out—by McNally 6 (Harrelson 2, Swoboda, Clendenon, Koosman 2); Watt 1 (Weis); Koosman 5 (Etchebarren, Blair, Powell, McNally, F. Robinson). Hits—off McNally 5 and 3 runs (3 earned) in 7 inns.; Watt 2 and 2 (1) in 1. Hit by Pitcher—McNally (Jones). Winning Pitcher—Koosman. Losing Pitcher—Watt. Time—2:14. Umpires—DiMuro (AL), Weyer (NL), Soar (AL), Secory (NL), Napp (AL), Crawford (NL). Attendance—57,397.

World Series Averages

BATTING

	G	AB	R	H	2B	3B	HR	RBI	BB	SO	SB-C	SH	SF	HB	E	AVG
Agee	5	18	1	3	0	0	1	1	2	5	1-0	0	0	0	0	.167
Boswell	1	3	1	1	0	0	0	0	0	0	0-0	0	0	0	0	.333
Charles	4	15	1	2	1	0	0	0	0	2	0-0	0	0	0	0	.133
Clendenon	4	14	4	5	1	0	3	4	2	6	0-0	0	0	0	0	.357
Dyer	1	1	0	0	0	0	0	0	0	0	0-0	0	0	0	0	.000
Garrett	2	1	0	0	0	0	0	0	2	1	0-0	1	0	0	1	.000
Gaspar	3	2	1	0	0	0	0	0	0	0	0-0	0	0	0	0	.000
Grote	5	19	1	4	2	0	0	1	1	3	0-0	0	0	0	0	.211
Harrelson	5	17	1	3	0	0	0	0	3	4	0-0	0	0	0	0	.176
Jones	5	19	2	3	1	0	0	0	1	1	0-0	0	0	1	0	.158
Kranepool	1	4	1	1	0	0	1	1	0	0	0-0	0	0	0	0	.250
Martin	1	0	0	0	0	0	0	0	0	0	0-0	1	0	0	0	.000
Shamsky	3	6	0	0	0	0	0	0	0	0	0-0	0	0	0	0	.000
Swoboda	4	15	1	6	1	0	0	1	1	3	0-1	0	0	0	0	.400
Weis	5	11	1	5	0	0	1	3	4	2	0-0	0	1	0	1	.455
Pitchers	—	14	0	2	2	0	0	2	0	8	0-0	0	0	0	0	.143
TOTAL	5	159	15	35	8	0	6	13	15	35	1-1	2	1	1	2	.220

Pinch-hitters: Dyer 0-1, Gaspar 0-1, Martin 0-0, Shamsky 0-2.

PITCHING

	G	GS	GC	W-L	IP	H	R	ER	BB	SO	HR	SHO	Saves	ERA
Cardwell	1	0	0	0-0	1	0	0	0	0	0	0	0	0	0.00
Gentry	1	1	0	1-0	6⅔	3	0	0	5	4	0	0	0	0.00
Koosman	2	2	1	2-0	17⅔	7	4	4	4	9	2	0	0	2.00
Ryan	1	0	0	0-0	2⅓	1	0	0	2	3	0	0	1	0.00
Seaver	2	2	1	1-1	15	12	5	5	3	9	1	0	0	3.00
Taylor	2	0	0	0-0	2⅓	0	0	0	1	3	0	0	1	0.00
TOTAL	5	5	2	4-1	45	23	9	9	15	28	3	1*	2	1.80

* Combined shutout (Gentry and Ryan).

Picture Credits